Journey into Holiness

Edited and with
an Introduction by
NORMAN G. WILSON

Wesleyan Publishing House
Indianapolis, Indiana

Copyright © 2000 by Wesleyan Publishing House
All Rights Reserved
Published by Wesleyan Publishing House
Indianapolis, Indiana 46250
Printed in the United States of America
ISBN 0-89827-215-7

Table of Contents

Introduction 9

Essence 13

  Who Is the Holy Spirit?
    William M. Greathouse 15

  Worshiping God's Holiness
    Robert E. Coleman 20

  Holiness Belongs to God
    Lee M. Haines 24

  The Holy Spirit's Goal
    Dan Tipton 26

  Life from a New Mind
    David L. Thompson 29

  Experiencing Holiness
    A. Wingrove Taylor 33

  Sanctified Vessels
    D. Wayne Brown 38

  The Baptism of the Holy Ghost
    Hannah Whitall Smith 41

  What Is Christian Perfection?
    John Wesley 47

  Progression in Holiness
    Joseph H. Smith 50

  What's in a Name?
    Robert W. McIntyre 53

Experience 57

  Questions and Answers about Sanctification
    Norman G. Wilson 59

Called to Imitate God
David Holdren 63

The Secret of Victorious Living
O.D. Emery 66

Godly Living in an Ungodly World
David Vardaman 68

Holiness for a New Millennium
John N. Oswalt 71

Samuel Logan Brengle: Holiness Evangelist
V. Raymond Edman 75

Rediscovering the Holiness of God
Steve DeNeff 80

Unconditional Surrender
J.D. Abbott 85

Two Sides of Holiness
Joe W. Colaw 88

Advice to the Not Yet Perfect
Clarence Bence 91

Effects 95

Reflecting the Holiness of God
Stan A. Toler 97

The More Excellent Way
Thomas H. Hermiz 101

Our Highest Priority
Thomas E. Armiger 105

The Power of Holiness
Bernard H. Phaup 108

What Is the Evidence of the Holy Spirit?
Alton J. Shea 111

Humility and Holiness
Andrew Murray 114

The Spiritual Edge: The Advantage of Sanctification
Jerry Brecheisen 118

Too Few Spirit-filled Christians!
Clyde C. Dupin 122

He Preached Holiness
Dow Chamberlain 125

Authentic Holiness at Home
Denis Applebee 130

Expression 133

Hope for the Holiness Message
Keith Drury 135

Incandescent Christians
George E. Failing 138

Preaching Holiness
David E. Wilson 141

The Gift of Pentecost—The Holy Spirit
Virgil A. Mitchell 144

Spiritual Channels That Run Deep
Harry Wood 147

The Disappearance of Sin
Earle L. Wilson 151

Empowered Witnesses
Paul S. Rees 153

How to Kill the Holiness Message
J.R. Mitchell 156

Holiness Is a Social Gospel
Marlin Hotle 159

Communicating Holiness Cross-Culturally
John Connor 161

Expectation 167

Hungering for Holiness
Roy S. Nicholson 169

A Plea and Prayer for Holiness
David S. Medders 174

Is It for Me?
Martha M. Evans 179

God's Call to Purity
Melvin H. Synder 181

The Imperative of Entire Sanctification
Wayne E. Caldwell 184

The Sanctification of Dr. E. Stanley Jones
Bernie Smith (compiler) 186

How Soon?
Wilbur T. Dayton 188

Clean Hands and a Pure Heart
Barry L. Ross 191

Acknowledgements

It has been said none of us is unique; we paste bits and pieces of others on ourselves. That is an apt description of this book. It is not the work of one author. It is, rather, the collective wisdom of many people pasted together into a beautiful collage called holiness.

I want to express my appreciation to the following:

To Don Cady, Laura Peterson, and the entire team at Wesleyan Publishing House for their help with this project.

To Andy Dayton, Becky James, Julie Alexander and Gail Whitmire for preparing the manuscript.

To Lawrence Wilson for editorial assistance.

To Jerry Brecheisen for creative insights, editorial assistance and manuscript oversight.

Introduction

The Psalmist said, *Blessed are those whose strength is in you, who have set their hearts on pilgrimage* (Psalm 84:5). The race to righteousness is intensifying. There is a new spiritual awakening by a twenty-first century crowd tired of the consequences of disobeying God's law. And this awakening crosses all generational fences.

Builders, "the greatest generation," in the words of one author, look for something to give them inner assurance, and growth in grace. Many of them have lived their three-score and ten, but they still long to "grow-up" in their faith, even as they watch their insurance policies come of age.

Baby Boomers by the score face new and challenging responsibilities as they reach their next level of maturity. They watch their children's families grow in a worrisome world. They face their own mortality as they tend their elderly parents. Their hectic pace adds a new level of weariness to their lives. But not all of that weariness is physical or emotional. Some of it goes to the very soul. They're tired of spiritual emptiness and half-hearted faith.

Generation X glaringly stands for the right in a world that glamorizes the wrong. They want a no-frills religion. They're more interested in the condition of the heart than the progress of the building fund. They want a steadfast belief to fill the aching void in their heart that hasn't been filled by the jingles of ten thousand advertisers.

The Millenials, today's teens, want something more than their big brothers and sisters had. A *Newsweek* magazine columnist calls their search a "revival of religion." But it's a revival unlike any other. Millenials are blending religious philosophies like articles of designer clothing to cover their spirit against the cold winds of time.

All told, it is an unprecedented search for God—a modern day hungering for holiness.

Those of the Wesleyan persuasion join the search. Their patriarch, John Wesley, knew both the awfulness of spiritual emptiness and the joyfulness of a whole surrender to the will of God.

But even for him, it was the result of a spiritual journey. He knew there were no quick fixes. Holiness is wholeness, as one definition says. The root of the word "holy" is also the root of the word "healthy." The apostle John wrote, *Dear friend, I pray that you may enjoy good health and that all may go well with you, even as your soul is getting along well* (3 John 2). Just as one would seek a healthier physical lifestyle, so there is a search for a healthier spiritual lifestyle.

That's why this book is so important. From the anointed pens of classic and contemporary pastors, educators, church leaders, and authors, you will discover some principles that can add spiritual power to your life.

Use these principles first in your own journey. Discover what "God has prepared for those who love Him." Whether you are a new Christian wondering about the next level of commitment or a seasoned saint looking for words and phrases to describe God's inner work in your heart, this book will help.

And then use these principles in your ministry to others—others who are on their own journey. These are teachable principles. They have been tested in the classroom of experience. The authors have made their own journey and have kept a journal that will be extremely helpful in your local church ministry. These are eternally important truths.

Preach them.

Teach them in the classroom

Discuss them in a small group setting.

Share them in a counseling session.

These are not words to be left on a shelf or displayed on a coffee table. They are principles to be learned and applied on the street where you live.

Read this book devotionally.

Read it resourcefully.

Read it expectantly.

But, most of all, read it with a heart that wants to be all that God intended.

Norman G. Wilson, Editor

Essence

Some things are easy to recognize, but difficult to describe. For instance, I have never heard a truly adequate definition of humor. Anyone can tell a joke. But it's hard to identify exactly what makes it funny. Humor is easy to see, hard to define.

Holiness is a bit like that. Most anyone can identify it. We know godliness when we see it. But to translate that quality into words is no simple task.

So what is the essence of holiness?

With precision and insight these writers have drawn a bead on that elusive target. In common terms they describe the hallmark of God's character—His holiness. We begin to see the Holy One—and we begin to understand His ancient command, *Be holy, because I am holy.*

And Can It Be?

And can it be that I should gain
an interest in the Savior's blood?
Died He for me, who caused His pain?
For me, who Him to death pursued?
Amazing love! How can it be
that Thou, my God, shouldst die for me?

He left His Father's throne above,
so free, so infinite His grace;
emptied Himself of all but love,
and bled for Adam's helpless race.
'Tis mercy all, immense and free,
for, O my God, it found out me.

Long my imprisoned spirit lay
fast bound in sin and nature's night;
Thine eye diffused a quickening ray.
I woke; the dungeon flamed with light!
My chains fell off; my heart was free.
I rose, went forth, and followed Thee.

No condemnation now I dread;
Jesus, and all in Him, is mine!
Alive in Him, my living Head,
and clothed in righteousness divine,
bold I approach the eternal throne,
and claim the crown, through Christ, my own.

—Charles Wesley

There is a joy that is deeper than human suffering, higher than the clouds, wider than the conflict, stronger than all opposing forces, stronger than all conditions. It comes from the heart of God. It is the joy of the Lord. It cannot be strangled by the enemy, nor crushed by the power of darkness. Its voice cannot be stilled by the tumult, nor swallowed up by the raging of the tempest. It is deeper, and higher, and sweeter than all, saying, "My beloved, I am with thee to keep thee in all thy ways." This is holiness.

—P. F. Bresee

Who Is the Holy Spirit?

by William M. Greathouse

No Christian with eyes and ears can deny that the winds of the Spirit are blowing with new force today—both upon the dry bones of the institutional church and also upon multitudes of Christians who look askance at the organized Church of Jesus Christ. Both the religious and secular press carry periodic reports of this surging of religious fervor, which is sweeping the land. Any attempt to evaluate *all* the manifestations of this phenomenon would surely miss significant features of this miracle.

The Holy Spirit is no longer "the unknown Person" of the Godhead. If the Protestant Reformation brought Christ back into the center of Christian faith, today's awakening is focusing attention upon the Spirit. Herein lie both the promise and the peril of this new movement.

The New Testament exhortation that we be filled with the Holy Spirit has found thousands of receptive hearts, not only among Protestants of various denominations and theological persuasions, but also among Roman Catholics. Literally thousands of these persons testify to the Spirit-filled life, and among these persons

Pentecost has been restored to its position as normative Christianity. What was once more or less the private emphasis of the holiness movement has now become much more fashionable, because our emphasis is similar, in many ways, to the position of Christians who live within widely differing theological traditions. What should be our response to this new situation?

Differences of Interpretation

First of all, we must recognize differences of interpretation, which distinguish advocates of the Spirit-filled life.

For example, Wesleyans believe that Pentecost brings heart purity and perfect love. Keswickians place emphasis upon the victory and power of Pentecost. Pentecostals and neo-charismatics see speaking in tongues as the sign of the Spirit's infilling.

Some of these distinctions are partly in the realm of emphasis and terminology, while others reach to the very heart of the Christian experience. In order to point up these distinctions, I shall attempt a thumbnail summary of each.

The Wesleyan View

From our Wesleyan perspective, the Pentecostal baptism with the Holy Spirit purges the heart of the believer from sin, perfects him in God's *agape* love, and thereby empowers him for effective Christian witness. We penitently acknowledge, however, that many of us have not paid the full price for such a genuinely Pentecostal experience. Too often, we have settled for a loveless, passionless profession of holiness which belies the New Testament.

Under the impact of the Spirit's moving in our times many of us who call ourselves Wesleyans are coming to see clearly that the heart of holiness is to be filled, cleansed, and indwelt by the Holy Spirit, and, further, that the baptism with the Spirit is a baptism of love. Some of us are becoming increasingly concerned that we relate Pentecost to evangelism, without modifying our historic insistence that the baptism with the Spirit personally connotes entire sanctification.

The Keswick View

Closely related to the Wesleyan teaching, and yet distinct from it at certain points, is the viewpoint associated with the famous Keswick Convention, which dates from 1875 in Keswick, England.

The Keswick teaching lays stress upon the Christian's being filled with the Spirit as essential to a life of spiritual victory and Christlikeness. Although these teachers stress the crucifixion of self and the cleansed life, they differ with Wesleyans as to the possibility of the destruction of sin in the believer's life. The indwelling Spirit is generally seen as counteracting the old nature, which remains until death.

In practical emphasis, however, the Keswick message is quite close to the Wesleyan. The difference may be more in words than in reality. For if a person has really died to sin and self, and has been truly baptized with the Holy Spirit, he is sanctified in the New Testament sense.

A great many of those who teach and profess the Spirit-filled life would come somewhere within this school of interpretation. One strength of this position is its strong emphasis upon the Christian's obligation to maintain a Spirit-filled relationship and to give a Spirit-filled witness to Christ.

The Pentecostal View

A third point of view is the Pentecostal, now being strongly urged also by the neo-Pentecostal and neo-charismatic advocates of the Spirit-filled life. Many Roman Catholic priests, nuns, and laypersons identify with this position, which until the early 1960s was largely limited to the small Pentecostal churches and sects.

Here the weight of stress is not upon the purifying or perfecting work of the Spirit baptism, but upon the personal and emotional aspects of this Pentecostal effusion and the accompanying evidences of tongues-speaking.

Whereas both the Wesleyan and Keswick schools see *holy love* as the one unmistakable evidence of the Spirit's full indwelling, the Pentecostal insists that speaking in tongues is the indisputable sign. The former places primary stress upon the graces of the Spirit, the latter upon His gifts.

These differences of emphasis generally lead to two entirely different concepts of the Spirit-filled life. Wesleyans and Keswickians place heavy stress on the *ethical* manifestations of the Spirit's presence. Pentecostals tend to over-emphasize *physical* manifestations.

Christ Is the Pattern of the Spirit-filled Life

His entire life, from the moment of His miraculous conception to the climactic moment when He offered Himself *through the eternal Spirit* (Hebrews 9:14) as our perfect sin offering, was a manifestation of the Holy Spirit. The Holy Spirit is, therefore, the *Christ*-Spirit, for "The fruits of the Spirit are the virtues of Christ," in Schleiermacher's fine phrase. God gave the Spirit *without limit* to Jesus (John 3:34) so that He becomes the norm of the Spirit-filled human life.

It was not until Jesus gave up His life forgivingly on the cross that the pattern was complete.

> *To this you were called, because Christ suffered for you, leaving you an example, that you should follow in His steps. "He committed no sin, and no deceit was found in His mouth." When they hurled their insults at Him, He did not retaliate; when He suffered, He made no threats. Instead, He entrusted Himself to Him who judges justly* (1 Peter 2:21-23).

Christ's Glorification Is the Absolute Condition of the Gift of the Spirit

At the Feast of Tabernacles, Jesus announced, *Whoever believes in Me . . . streams of living water will flow from within him* (John 7:38). John immediately comments, *By this He meant the Spirit, whom those who believed in Him were later to receive* (v. 39).

The Spirit was active through the ancient dispensation. Yet the New Testament says unequivocally: the *Holy Spirit* was not given until Christ was glorified—that is, not until after the Crucifixion, Resurrection, and Ascension.

Peter makes this clear in his Pentecostal sermon: *God has raised this Jesus to life, and we are all witnesses of the fact. Exalted to the right hand of God, He has received from the Father the promised Holy Spirit and has poured out what you now see and hear* (Acts 2:32-33).

Who is the Holy Spirit? He is the Spirit of Christ. He is self-effacing. He does not speak of Himself, but of Christ. His work is to reveal Christ *in* us and *through* us. Any concept of spirituality that promises some advance beyond Christlikeness through the indwelling Spirit is spurious.

Christian perfection is a spiritual constellation made up of these gracious stars—perfect repentance, perfect faith, perfect humility, perfect meekness, perfect self-denial, perfect resignation, perfect hope, perfect charity for our visible enemies, as well as for our earthly relations; and, above all, perfect love for our invisible God, through the explicit knowledge of our Mediator Jesus Christ. And as this last star is always accompanied by all the others, as Jupiter is by his satellites, we frequently use, as St. John, the phrase perfect love instead of the word "perfection"; and understanding by it the pure love of God, shed abroad in the heart of established believers by the Holy Ghost, which is abundantly given them under the fullness of the Christian dispensation.

—John Fletcher

Worshiping God's Holiness

by Robert E. Coleman

The poet, Carlyle, wrote, "Let me make a nation's songs, and I care not who makes their laws." His point is well taken, for those things we spontaneously sing about have a way of shaping our minds, just as they reveal what is uppermost in our thoughts.

That's why, in my quiet moments of meditation and prayer, I like to join the choirs of heaven and, as it were, sing along with that vast worshiping host gathered about the throne of God. The words of their songs are recorded in the Book of Revelation, beginning in chapter four and continuing intermittently through chapter nineteen. These doxologies express the deepest desires of those who, with unveiled faces, have seen the Lord in His glory. If we would learn to sing with them, they could teach us the values of the New Jerusalem. I know of no more uplifting exercise to the soul.

The anthems begin with the celestial creatures unceasingly exclaiming, *Holy, holy, holy is the Lord God Almighty, Who was, and is, and is to come* (4:8). It is an affirmation that God is self-existent and separate from all other beings, and also utterly undefiled by any impurity in His nature. This Holy One, sovereign of the universe, stands above time, with no beginning or ending, no past or future, always the same.

As the awesome song of the cherubim swells through the courts of heaven, the white-robed elders fall down and worship Him who lives forever, saying, *You are worthy, our Lord and God, to receive glory and honor and power, for You created all things, and by Your will they were created and have their being* (4:11). The hymn attests the incomparable worthiness of Him by whose pleasure all things have their being.

The creatures about the throne then unite to sing of the Lord who has redeemed the world by His blood (5:9-10). It is called a *new song* because that which Christ has accomplished is wholly different and superior to the old covenant. No sooner have they concluded than myriads of angels lift their voices in antiphonal praise, declaring, *Worthy is the Lamb, Who was slain, to receive power and wealth and wisdom and strength and honor and glory and praise!* (5:12). Reaching a climax, *every creature in heaven and on earth and under the earth and on the sea, and all that is in them,* join the refrain, saying, "*To Him Who sits on the throne and to the Lamb be praise and honor and glory and power, for ever and ever!*" (5:13). Left breathless in wonder, unable to find words to convey any higher adoration, the living creatures simply keep repeating, *Amen!* while the four-and-twenty elders fall down and worship the Everlasting King (5:14).

With the cosmic triumph of Christ resounding throughout eternity, Revelation then, and only then, proceeds to describe the events that are actually to transpire before the consummation of the Kingdom (6:1-17). It is a woeful story of one calamity after another in an accelerating sequence of judgments upon the earth. Yet, at decisive points through the unfolding narrative, the scene shifts briefly to heaven, and John sees the worshiping hosts about the throne of God.

A Longing Cry

Each recurring scene further amplifies His praise. A longing cry to the Lord *holy and true* is heard from those who have been martyred for their testimony, after the breaking of the fifth seal (6:10). Again, before the final seal is removed from the book of destiny, the Revelator has a vision of heaven, in which *a great multitude that no one could count, from every nation, tribe, people and language,* are seen about the throne, *wearing white robes and... holding palm branches in their hands* (7:9). They cry out with a loud voice, *Salvation belongs to our God, Who sits on the throne, and to the Lamb* (7:10). At their shout, all the angels prostrate themselves before the throne and worship God in another ascription of blessing (7:12).

Assured that the Great Commission will be fulfilled, the account of the coming tragedies upon the earth continues until the seventh trumpet sounds. Then *great voices* are heard again in heaven, declaring the certainty of the Savior's rule: *The kingdom of the world has become the kingdom of our Lord, and of His Christ, and He will reign for ever and ever* (11:15). This song leads to the elders falling on their faces and offering to God their praise for His invincible power, vindicating truth and justice, and the honor of His Son (11:17, 18).

A Shout of Victory

A shout of victory is heard again from heaven in the next chapter, reminding the harassed church on earth that salvation has come, and that Satan has been cast down. Therefore, God's people should rejoice, realizing that, in Christ, they are more than conquerors (12:10-12).

The ensuing tale of the mortally wounded Devil, in the rage of defeat, bringing the greater part of mankind under his mark, prompts another vision of the throne and the praise of the Lamb (14:1-5). Angels appear with proclamations to earthlings, the first being a summons to give glory to God (14:6, 7). Then, before the seven last plagues are poured out, the praise service about the throne is described in detail, and those who have been faithful join in singing the song of Moses and of the Lamb (15:3, 4).

There follows in rapid succession the unleashing of God's terrifying wrath upon the rebellious world. The end has come. But when it is all over, the sound of jubilant singing breaks through the smoking pall at fallen Babylon. A great multitude is heard in heaven, shouting, *"Hallelujah! Salvation and glory and power belong to our God, for true and just are His judgments. He has condemned the great prostitute who corrupted the earth by her adulteries. He has avenged on her the blood of his servants."* And again they shouted: *"Hallelujah!"* (19:1-3). The elders and cherubim, always sensitive to the honor of God, catch up the shout, falling down and worshiping Him that sat on the throne, saying, *"Amen, Hallelujah!"* (19:4).

A Voice from the Throne

A voice comes from the throne, calling upon the people to adore Him, a message that reaches down to us across the ages. *Praise our God, all you His servants, you who fear Him, both small and great!* (19:5). Perhaps an angel, seeing the oppressed Church still on earth, wanted to help us get our priorities in order. For whatever our rank or station, the worship of God should be our fondest occupation. Nothing is more enabling to the soul. When we magnify His name and celebrate His glory, we ourselves partake of greatness.

Imagine the crescendo of heaven's hosts, unrestrained by any selfish inhibitions, united as a single voice of adoration to God. It is likened to *the roar of rushing waters and like loud peals of thunder,* shouting, *"Hallelujah! For Lord our God Almighty reigns."* (19:6). He, not Caesar, rules in undisputed control. Yet, wonder of wonders, this great Potentate, the King of glory, the Lord God omnipotent, is *our* God—He is personally related to His people, so that we are His, and He is ours.

Enraptured with the contemplation of this blessing, members of the heavenly throng exhort themselves, *Let us rejoice and be glad and give Him glory! For the wedding of the Lamb has come, and His bride has made herself ready* (19:7). At last, the sacrificial Savior will gather His Church to Himself in eternal wedlock. *Fine linen, bright and clean, was given her to wear (Fine linen stands for the righteous acts of the saints)* (19:8).

How fitting that the songs of heaven should close on this note. They began with the recognition of a God thrice holy in His nature; now they close with the display of His holiness in the righteous acts of His Church.

For our part, we should be getting ready to meet Him when He comes. Where the Spirit shows our garments to be soiled by uncleanness, we must do something about it. Thanks to His grace, when there is honest confession of sin, He is faithful to forgive and cleanse us from all unrighteousness. However limited may be our comprehension of His will, He expects us to give all that we know of ourselves to all that we understand of Him—to love and trust Him with all that we are, all that we hope to be.

This is the reality in which the Christian lives. Though our bodies are still held by the earth, our spirits can soar with the angels in the city of unceasing song. There, we are at home. In the inner sanctuary of our beings, we are already beginning to know something of that praise in which the King of heaven dwells. And the singing grows sweeter with the years.

Holiness Belongs to God

by Lee M. Haines

Holiness is a word that prompts a wide range of responses. To some, it is a code word that serves as a call to arms to defend a theological position. To some, it is a threatening word that demands the impossible. For others, it is a word that conjures up memories of bondage inflicted by others. For still others, it is a word that brings painful memories of repeated failures.

Holiness Is More

Holiness is really much more and much better than any of these meanings. It is a key word in describing the nature of God. The word belongs uniquely to Him. It separates Him from everything else and from everyone else. It is an indispensable word for speaking about God.

In Revelation 15:4a, the saints are singing, *Who will not fear You, O Lord, and bring glory to Your name? For You alone are holy.* In Isaiah 40:25, the Lord said, *To whom will you compare Me? Or who is My equal?* In 1 Samuel 6:20, the men of Beth Shemesh said, *Who can stand in the presence of the Lord, this holy God?* In Hosea 11:9, the Lord said, *I am God, and not man—the Holy One among you.* And in Isaiah 57:15, again, *For this is what the high and lofty One says—He Who lives forever, Whose name is holy: "I live in a high and holy place."* I cannot encounter God without encountering His holiness. I cannot know Him without becoming aware of His holiness. I cannot have a relationship with Him except in the context of His holiness. God and holiness are inseparable.

But God's holiness is not a barrier to our having a loving relationship. Holiness does not eternally separate Him from me. Holiness belongs to God. I, too, can belong to God. And in that way holiness and I can belong together. Impossible? Unreasonable? Self-contradictory? To man's limited understanding, yes.

Holiness Brings Partnership

The truth is that God longs to share His holiness with me. In 2 Peter 1:4, the apostle tells us that God enables us to *participate in the divine nature.* In Isaiah 57:15 (see above), the Lord speaks of His own lofty abode, but goes on to say, *I live in a high and holy place, but also with him who is contrite and lowly in spirit.* And in Hosea 11:9 (see above), the Lord distinguishes Himself from man, particularly at the point of His mercy: *I will not carry out My fierce anger, nor will I turn and devastate Ephraim. For I am God, and not man—the Holy One among you. I will not come in wrath.*

I was not quite ten years old when the Lord first began to reveal to me the vast difference between His holiness and my sinfulness. I was already committed to being His minister. But now we came to the heart of the matter. I was appalled at what He showed me of selfishness and willfulness and stubbornness within. The harder I struggled to free myself, the lower I sank. But then I recognized that He was inviting me, not rejecting me. And just after my tenth birthday, I said yes to His love and mercy. Later, I consecrated my all to Him and He cleansed and filled me with His Spirit.

And yet today He reveals long-established habits of work and relationship that need to be refined to properly display His holiness —and He brings it about. Holiness belongs to God—but so do I. And He can make us belong together.

The Holy Spirit's Goal

by Dan Tipton

The work and ministry of the Holy Spirit so intertwine the life of a Christian that the two should be indistinguishable. He is the constant companion of the saint. His objectives include helping each Christian realize and live up to all the provisions wrought by Christ at Calvary, guiding each person into full experience of the promises of God's Word, and bringing each believer into complete possession of the privileges of being a child of God. The Holy Spirit is not a spiritual babysitter. He has clear objectives for every Christian personally, and for the Body of Christ, the Church, collectively. He is not idle. He takes no vacations. He doesn't even take breaks while on the job. He actively perfects the will of God in all Christians.

The challenge for the Christian is to work in full cooperation with the Holy Spirit. The pinnacle truth in God's Word concerning the provisions, promises, and privileges provided for the Christian reveals that any person can be so reconciled to God that it can be said that person is entirely sanctified. This simple statement is loaded with theological truth. It summarizes the height, depth, and breadth of Christian experience. Entire sanctification in the heart and life of a Christian becomes the goal of the Holy Spirit. Neglecting this objective or diminishing its priority places one out of step, out of harmony, even dangerously close to thwarting the ultimate effort of the Holy Spirit to bring glory to God within the life of the Christian.

A State of Holiness

What does entire sanctification mean? Both the words *entire* and *sanctification* contribute significant spiritual realities. The word *sanctify* and its derivative, *sanctification*, are used to describe the act and process whereby a state or condition of holiness is realized. In the

26

Old Testament, the concept found clear expression by a twofold application. To be sanctified or made holy, something or someone had first to be separated from anything that was a source of contamination or that was unholy. Having been so separated it was next set apart unto God and dedicated or devoted to Him alone. This is illustrated in many ways in Old Testament passages. The Sabbath day was sanctified. The temple, the tabernacle, the priestly garments, the altars and even certain geographic places were sanctified.

The New Testament builds powerfully on this truth. Sanctification in the New Testament emphasizes that the human heart can be made clean, pure, and free from the contamination of the carnal mind and nature. The heart can be set aside in devotion and consecration to God. Sanctification, in this perspective, means to make clean or holy in an ethical, moral sense with a resulting consecration of oneself fully, without reservation, whatever the cost, to God. Sanctification is the process and crisis by which such inner cleansing and renewal takes place.

The Holy Spirit's Work

One important aspect of the work of the Holy Spirit in the sanctification of the believer is the cleansing impact upon the heart. The problem of sin in humanity is twofold. Sin may be defined as those willful acts of disobedience to God's will, way, and law. These violations against God separate a person from Him and justly bring eternal condemnation. God graciously provided a means for our salvation through the redeeming, atoning sacrifice of Christ. His death on Calvary and triumphant resurrection supplied the means whereby the sins of each person can be forgiven. A personal relationship with God awaits any person who, by faith in Jesus Christ, comes to God. The problem of transgression can be forgiven through Christ's provision, which the Holy Spirit makes known to us and applies to us, as well.

The problem of sin is more than transgression. Sin is also defined as a condition of the heart that needs to be cleansed. A rebellious resistance to God remains within the heart of each convert. The new Christian finds his pathway toward a mature spiritual life challenged by an inborn problem that seeks to reject God's way with a self-enthroning alternative. As each Christian grows in grace and matures in the Christian life, a growing awareness of this inner conflict develops. Eventually this matter produces a consciousness or inner feeling of contamination, of being unclean, of needing something more of God's work. The ministry of the Holy Spirit seeks to produce just such an awareness. The heart of the Christian cries out for purity, for cleansing, for oneness with God. A hunger and thirst for righteousness prevails. The Christian bows before God in total submission, consecrating and committing to be a living sacrifice unto God. It is then that the Holy Spirit instantaneously cleanses the heart from the rebellious, carnal nature, sets the heart apart unto God, and indwells the heart as a fit dwelling or temple where His residence is welcomed and wanted. The Holy Spirit gives a new empowering for victorious, godly living.

Entire Sanctification

When such a moment comes in the heart of the Christian, it is then that entire sanctification becomes reality. The word *entire* implies that sanctification, in some sense, was already present for and in the Christian, though less than entire, prior to that moment. Remember, the definition of sanctification means the setting apart *from* anything that was a source of contamination and the setting apart *unto* God. In a very real way, this setting apart began at conversion. It reached a state of completion when the Holy Spirit cleansed the heart from the rebellious spirit of the carnal nature. When someone becomes a Christian, it is said, in theological terms, that he has experienced *initial* sanctification. When the Holy Spirit cleanses the heart, it is said that a person has experienced *entire* sanctification.

This is the goal that the Holy Spirit wants to achieve in the heart of every Christian. When this truth lacks clarity and strong emphasis in the pulpits, the church classrooms, in the songs, testimonies, and altar calls of the Church, then the Church and her leaders have lessened their cooperation with the Holy Spirit's work and ministry. It is God's plan for every Christian to fully experience the provisions, promises, and privileges provided through Christ at Calvary—entire sanctification. Therefore (in the words of the Hebrew author), *we must pay more careful attention . . . to what we have heard, so that we do not drift away* (Hebrews 2:1). Our involvement with the work and ministry of the Holy Spirit depends upon this. Entire sanctification is God's will and plan.

Life from a New Mind

Paul's Notes on Christian Holiness

by David L. Thompson

Using mind-value categories instead of the doctrinal terms familiar to the holiness movement, Paul investigates Christian holiness in Romans 12:1–15:6. The structure of the book brings the entire treatise to focus here. And the focus is on a call to self-surrender. The conformity to worldliness at the core of our being is replaced by a life that is holy, acceptable to God—no small miracle!

To the Christian community at Rome, Paul presents what Wesley later called Christian perfection or entire sanctification. Paul does it in terms of a deep, decisive, life-directing change of mind. He wrote the answer in these mind-value categories because he saw the problem in those terms. Along with other biblical writers, Paul defined "worldliness" (carnality) primarily as a way of thinking. It is a set of values that is centered in oneself—a mindset which, even in Christians, serves self, subordinates commitment to convenience, and submits devotion to natural desire.

John described this mindset as governed by bodily desires, enamored with trinkets, and buried in the rat race of making a living (1 John 2:15-17). Some characteristic attitudes of this mindset are jealousy, hostility, contention, and pride—bedrock values of pagan life. All so natural! Christians with this mindset are *just like other people,* said Paul (1 Corinthians 3:1-3). Christians they are, but not yet radically altered in the basic mindset from which they live.

A Comprehensive Change of Mind

Romans 12:1–15:6 shows the sweeping change of mindset envisioned for these Christians. In 12:3-8, we are asked to change our minds about ourselves, to head toward a realistic appraisal of ourselves in view of God's grace. Released both from false humility and pride, which short-circuit edifying ministry, we are freed to use with abandon whatever gifts God has given us.

In 12:9-13, we are asked to change our minds about others, particularly those in the Christian fellowship. We are to live out non-hypocritical love in an aggressive, prayerful, hopeful ministry of hospitality and Christian caring. In 12:14-21, we are asked to change our minds about our enemies. Getting even at all levels is displaced by approaches to conflict that overcome evil with good.

In 13:1-7, Paul takes up the matter of our relationships with government officials, addressing the more basic question of submission to authority. We are asked to have a change of mind about how we relate to those whose task it is to supervise our lives, to tell us what to do. In 13:8-10, we are asked to change our minds about love. Here is the key to the new mindset. We discover that love is central to the Christian's values, not peripheral or incidental. It is the very essence of holy living. We are asked, in 13:11-14, to change our minds about commitment, to set aside lethargy and service by convenience, and to realize that—like it or not—some matters require attention now, not tomorrow.

Finally, we are asked to change our minds about the nature and importance of personal convictions in 14:1–15:6. We are informed that the well-being of people is more important than our personal convictions, and that ministering to one another in love has priority over both our liberty and our restrictions. God is far more interested in our attitude toward the people with whom we disagree than He is with our particular set of convictions. Strength is defined in terms of loving liberty, not in terms of strict convictions.

Far from being miscellaneous admonitions, the paragraphs in Romans 12:1–15:6 give the very reasons why Christians are urged to give themselves to God as a living sacrifice (12:1-2) in so complete a surrender as to bring about a whole new way of thinking about self, others, and God. Why? Note the conjunction at the beginning of 12:3. *Because* we are asked to change our basic approach to ourselves, to others, to enemies, to authority, to the centrality of love, to the meaning of commitment, to the place of personal convictions—*because of these* challenges we are told to give ourselves to God who will make it possible!

A Critical Change of Mind

The tense of the verb, *to offer,* in Romans 12:1 shows that Paul has in mind a deliberate act of surrender. The sanctified life involves continuing surrender, to be sure, but that is not the first concern here. The call is first to an act of surrender that is so thoughtful and so pervasive as to set the course for all subsequent surrenders. As with the Old Testament sacrifice, upon which Paul's metaphor is based, there is a time when the sacrifice is done without reservation.

This change of mind is the key to the repeated demonstration in life that God's will is indeed "good, acceptable, and perfect." Repeated confrontation with our own selfishness in the attempt to live out God's will lead us finally to this altar of sacrifice. In that surrender, and in God's hallowing of the sacrifice, the selfish mindset is so broken that we can demonstrate on a continuing basis that God's will is good in the highest sense of the word.

A Continuing Change of Mind

The call is to self-surrender, not to self-destruction. The sacrifice lives! We surrender our selfishness, but are given the gift of the renewed self, freed to choose the mind of Christ. And choose we must! No level of Christian piety produces automatic Christians who are holy and loving without choice. So in 12:2, Paul directs the imperatives to the Roman Christians and not to God: *Do not conform any longer to the pattern of this world, but live transformed by the renewing of your mind.*

The sins that lurk as the antitheses of the positive admonitions of chapters 12–15 are sins of the mind: selfish attitudes. One must ask what it means to be tempted to pride, jealousy, hate, retaliation or rebelliousness. These temptations are different from the lure to commit an overt act of sin like theft.

The temptation to be jealous, for instance, is not an act, nor is it merely an abstract consideration of jealousy. It is, rather, the awareness that we are being drawn to jealousy, the awareness of jealousy rising within ourselves. At that moment, we are faced with the choice. In the power of Christ's Spirit, we can choose love, instead. We are called to it and empowered for it. In so doing, we bring to a halt, in that specific case, the world's attempt to squeeze us into its mold, and experiences the continuing renewal of the mind. That is the habit of the "living sacrifice."

A Cooperative Change of Mind

While some passages focus on God's role in the sanctifying process (1 Thessalonians 5:23; Acts 15:8), Paul here focuses on the believer's role in entering and living the new mind. Believers are to bring their total person as a living sacrifice, an act of worship centering in the mind. Believers are charged with halting conformity to the world and being transformed. In effect, *we* are to change *our* minds deeply, decisively, comprehensively, and continually. We alter our basic way of viewing God, others, and ourselves. It is at least that.

But there is much more than that. Already, in Romans 8, Paul has set all of the Christian's victory in the context of the dynamic life of God's Spirit. And here in 12:2, the second imperative is grammatically passive. We are not transforming ourselves. We are *being* transformed by the power of God. As we change our minds about the basic values out of which we will live our lives, God changes our minds. He will not do it without our continuing choice, and we cannot do it by ourselves. Together, we actually live moment by moment out of a mindset that shatters conformity to pagan values at every level of our lives and utterly transforms all our ways.

Experiencing Holiness

by A. Wingrove Taylor

I t is God's will that we experience holiness. It is the endearing experience—for to experience holiness is to experience the Holy One. Holiness is nothing neither less nor more than radical, royal, reliable, remarkable romance with the Redeemer.

Let's look at the vital high places of experiencing holiness. We cannot, of course, cover them. We can only make some comments about them. Although fundamental faith is a high place, we shall omit it in this study. I trust that the glory of the high places to be considered will naturally activate the glory of believing. The first high place of experiencing holiness is what I am calling *birthing*.

Birthing

I am referring, of course, to being born again—to the new birth. The birth of Isaac is a wonderful, biblical, and practical example of birthing (Galatians 4:22-23, 29 and John 3:36). God brought Isaac to birth in spite of debate, doubt, derision, death—of a womb—and dysfunction—of the reproductive systems (Genesis 15:1-4; 17:15-19; 18:9-14; 21:1-7). Paul has his own striking presentation of Abraham's hopeless situation (Romans 4:18-21). God used the most extreme situation to show His mercy and His might. All this says that any of us, whatever our situation, can experience birthing, for Abraham is the father of us all (Romans 4:16).

Birthing begins with loving Him Who is the Wonderful, and ends with loving the world (1 John 2:15-16). John 3:16 is a love verse. The birthing of eternal life, which is the end result of God's love, produces in us the love of God and love for God and for others (1 John 4:7).

Burying

The next high place of experiencing holiness is *burying*. Burying refers to the seed falling into the ground and dying (John 12:24). For me, it is one of the fine presentations of entire sanctification. In Jesus' discourse with Nicodemus we have the *truly, truly* of the new birth (John 3:3). In John 12:24, we have the *truly, truly* of the new death. I use burying as synonymous with "dead" and "crucified." We are to give most of our time to burying and the high place that follows it, because they are so crucial.

Burying may seem more like a horrible place than a high place. There is longing for rest and peace and, often, seeking the Lord alone in tears. But there is, I believe, both an easier and a truer way to victory. Burying is not a horrible place. It is indeed a high place. It is so because burying is very much related to radical romance with the Redeemer. As birthing brings us into eternal life in the Redeemer, so burying makes exclusive life with the Redeemer gloriously possible.

In the inspired word of God, Paul uses a legal and matrimonial illustration to highlight the high place of burial and death (Romans 7:1-4). The picture of burying here is beautiful. Christ uttered the concession of divorce in human matrimonial relationship, but for Himself, in spiritual relationship, He never utilizes it. With Christ, it is death and only death that is first and final. Our relationship with all spiritual suitors or spouses must terminate, through death, before He will establish absolute relationship with us.

The Romans passage refers to the spouse in Jewish Law. Other suitors or spouses can be sin (Romans 6:6-11), society (Galatians 6:14), maybe even the saints (1 Corinthians 2:2). The chief, all-encompassing rival spouse is self (Galatians 2:20). The self we are to be freed from by death is not the first and true self, fashioned in God's image. It is a foreign self, fashioned after the satanic spirit, grasping hopelessly to be God. It, therefore, manifests pride, anger, frustration, suspicion, and jealousy. It is false self that can and must be denied (Luke 9:23).

To deliver us from rival suitors, He Himself has already paid the price and made the sacrifice. He Himself took the cross and bore all the hardness of death. *We see Jesus,* say the Scriptures, who did *taste death for everyone* (Hebrews 2:9). He has experienced the grief of death so that, by dying with Him, we may experience the grace and even the glory of death.

Belonging

Burying brings us to the next high place in experiencing holiness. It is *belonging*. The concept of belonging comes from holiness and its very extensive word family. Throughout the Bible, the word family of holiness includes words such as chaste, clear, consecrate, dedicate, hallow, holy, holiest, holiness, pure, purification, purify, purity, saints, sanctification, sanctify, and sanctuary.

The holiness word family carries two distinctive meanings. One is possession—that is, belonging (Leviticus 20:26). The other is purification. Some Christians stress the possession application of holiness. Others stress purification. Maybe it is altogether my fault, but in my many years in the holiness movement, I have known only the purification emphasis. But the biblical record strongly supports both emphases. Rightly and radically belonging to God is the most spiritually revolutionizing reality that I have experienced in recent years.

Belonging is radical in its extensiveness—extensiveness of domain. The possession or belonging takes in not only the spirit (our upward and spiritual capacities) and the soul (our inward and social capacities), but also the body (our earthward and physical capacities) (1 Thessalonians 5:23). We are to love the One to whom we belong, freshly—with the heart, fundamentally—with the soul, forcefully—with might and strength, and intellectually—with the mind and understanding (Deuteronomy 6:5; Matthew 22:37; Mark 12:30; Luke 10:27).

Deuteronomy adds to extensiveness of domain, extensiveness of deeds. Belonging includes not only extensively loving the Lord, but also extensively following Him (Deuteronomy 1:36), fearing Him (4:10), seeking Him (4:29) and serving Him (10:12).

Belonging, or possession, is to be radical not only in its extensiveness, but also in its exclusiveness. Body, soul, spirit, heart, might, strength, mind, and understanding are to belong exclusively to God in all parts with no part lacking (1 Thessalonians 5:23; Matthew 22:37; Mark 12:30, 33; and Luke 10:27).

In 1 Thessalonians 5:23, there is the adverb *through and through*. This means completely and entirely. This is exclusiveness in degree.

This idea climaxes with the thought of exclusiveness in duration. It carries the meaning of belonging to God to the very end. This is saying to God, "forsaking all others, we keep ourselves only to You so long as. . . ." The song "Now I Belong to Jesus," says that "so long as" is "Not for the years of time alone but for eternity."

The soul must not draw back in the face of such extensiveness and exclusiveness of belonging to God. The plan of the Creator is that only out of full and unrivaled love and belonging to Him will come fruitful and unlimited love and belonging to ourselves or others.

A little boy was deeply worried about God's claim upon the exclusive love of his father. The father wisely answered, "It's like this, son. If I love only you, there may come a day when I will no longer love you. But if I love God with all of my love, there will never come a day when I will no longer love you."

Blessing

In the sequence of the high places of experiencing holiness, we come now to *blessing*. Blessing is directly linked to belonging. We seek early for blessing, but its true order is after burying and belonging. God's response to all belonging is all blessing (Ephesians 1:3).

The first blessing is the Almighty (Genesis 28:3-4; John 17:35, 19-23). In Christ, we die to all other suitors and commit ourselves to belong to God alone. Immediately, the Almighty, the all-powerful and sufficient One, comes in His fullness, dismisses any unwilling, previous suitors, and takes His rightful and natural place as our supreme Lover. His is the greatest blessing, for He Himself is the Blesser!

Another blessing is assurance (see Acts 15:8). What is the assurance that one is entirely sanctified? Some saints have varying versions. I like the two *truly*s. There are the two witnesses (Romans 8:16). God the Spirit always witnesses to our spirits.

A beautiful blessing is affections. These are, of course, the affections of Christ (Colossians 3:2-3; Galatians 5:22-26). A very practical blessing is answers (John 14:26). The Teacher has all of the answers, and if we have the Teacher, we will have the answers. And there are other blessings such as authority, anointing, articulation, and ability.

Becoming

There is one other high place of holiness that is imperative to consider. It is *becoming*. My own heart is very satisfied about the "second crisis," which is entire sanctification. But perhaps we need to recognize two errors. One is that as holiness denominations, we have been devout about purity to the tragic dwarfing of possession. The other is equally tragic. We have majored on the crisis of getting entirely sanctified, but have marginalized the continued growth of entire sanctification.

The analogy of marriage is very fitting. We get married in a moment of commitment, but it takes a lifetime to learn to live with one's spouse. It is similar with entire sanctification, though, of course, much more profound. There is a perfection of commitment and cleansing in a moment. It takes a lifetime, however, of learning to perfect the perfection (2 Corinthians 7:1).

There is a crying need for this doctrine of holiness to be demonstrated—not as human and hollow, not as harsh and hypocritical, not as hyped-up on one hand, nor humdrum on the other—but as holy, hearty, and helpful. The world is ripe for the golden day of holiness. Holiness that is a radical, royal, reliable, remarkable romance with the Redeemer is available for each of us. Some may need a "download," some an "upgrade." Heaven is ready to give to all who, on God's terms, will receive the Holy One and His holiness.

Sanctified Vessels

by D. Wayne Brown

In a large house there are articles not only of gold and silver, but also of wood and clay; some are for noble purposes and some for ignoble. If a man cleanses himself from the latter, he will be an instrument for noble purposes, made holy, useful to the Master and prepared to do any good work (2 Timothy 2:20-21).

Conditions that exist in the fellowship of believers are of great concern to the Lord. St. Paul uses the expression "large house" in describing the structure of this relationship, and may have been thinking about our Lord's words on the occasion when He was cleansing the Temple, as recorded in Matthew 21:13: *"It is written," He said to them, "'My house will be called a house of prayer,' but you are making it a 'den of robbers.'"*

Paul's figure of speech depicts a king's house or a wealthy man's dwelling. In it are vessels of gold, silver, wood, and earth, all of which are illustrative of people in the church—some honorable, some dishonorable. A distinction is made between the comparative lasting value of gold and silver, vessels over the more perishable wood and clay ones. There is also the beauty of gold and silver compared to wood and clay. The text speaks of sanctified vessels, further described as honorable, and the process by which this sanctification takes place.

Vessels that Are Separated

Paul states in Galatians 6:14, *May I never boast except in the cross of our Lord Jesus Christ, through which the world has been crucified to me, and I to the world.* This is a separation from the world of sin unto a special, God-centered purpose.

Each disciple is to live, not in an isolation of non-productivity, but rather in a desire to practice a radiant relationship with Christ and a multitude of "honorable vessels." There is great strength in being a part of a holy union where the multiplication of believers is the normal result of separated and sanctified human vessels working toward a holy purpose.

Vessels that Are Sanctified

The Apostle Paul prays an interesting prayer, which is recorded in 1 Thessalonians 5:23: *May God Himself, the God of peace, sanctify you through and through. May your whole spirit, soul and body be kept blameless at the coming of our Lord Jesus Christ.*

How can a cleansing or sanitizing of a human being be more all-inclusive than that which takes in spirit, soul and body? The thoroughness of this sanctification is so effective as to render the believer "blameless" before God. No wonder that Jesus said, *Blessed are the pure in heart, for they will see God* (Matthew 5:8).

We must not forget that the separation from the world-spirit of sin is an act on our part. But the work of sanitizing and cleansing the human heart is an act of God.

Vessels Equipped for a Purpose

The Scripture says that these honorable and sanctified vessels are *useful to the Master.*

Who will use these gold and silver vessels? Who is to receive glory from the utility of any or all of their gifts? The answer is, the Master. The word *master* speaks of an absolute ruler who requires the submission of our entire volitional nature. That sanctified vessel is anxious also to do the whole will of the Master. Such a vessel becomes a usable, pliable, and delightful tool with no purpose but to be used of the Master. It is consecrated.

The Beauty of the Vessels

The language here is expressive of ornamentation, beauty, and attractiveness when it speaks of vessels of gold and silver. We read a special command in Psalm 29:2: *Worship the Lord in the splendor of His holiness.*

God created our world and other worlds so massively beyond our comprehension that all we can do is strain our minds in thinking about the greatness of God. But God's creation of worlds holds no comparison with the greatness of His plan of salvation, which provides for the redemption of men—His created vessels.

May we, as His chosen vessels, not grieve the Holy Spirit by failing to avail ourselves of that beauty of holiness so generously provided by a loving heavenly Father.

I have learned that true Christianity consists, not in a set of options, or of forms and ceremonies, but in holiness of heart and life.

—John Wesley

The Baptism of the Holy Ghost

by Hannah Whitall Smith

(Abridged from the Christian classic,
The Christian's Secret of a Happy Life)

The baptism of the Holy Spirit is the crowning and vital point in all Christian experience, and right views concerning it are of very great importance. In considering it, two questions only need to be settled: What or Who is the Holy Ghost? And, what is it to be baptized with the Holy Ghost?

Who Is the Holy Ghost?

The Holy Ghost or Holy Spirit is simply God's Spirit. It is the life and power and nature of God, manifested in a spiritual way to man's spirit. It is, in fact, God Himself, as a spirit, communicating with the spiritual part of man's nature. (See John 14:16-23.)

You, however, are controlled not by the sinful nature but by the Spirit, if the Spirit of God lives in you. And if anyone does not have the Spirit of Christ, he does not belong to Christ. But if Christ is in you, your body is dead because of sin, yet your spirit is alive because of righteousness. And if the Spirit of Him Who raised Jesus from the dead is living in you, He Who raised Christ from the dead will also give life to your mortal bodies through His Spirit, Who lives in you (Romans 8:9-11).

The different expressions used here all mean, of course, the same thing: *the Spirit, the Spirit of Christ, Christ in you . . . the Spirit of Him who raised up Jesus* all mean evidently the Holy Spirit. If we substitute the words "life" or "nature" for Spirit, we shall perhaps be helped to understand just what the Holy Spirit is. As we read in Romans 8:2, *the law of the Spirit of life set me free from the law of sin and death.*

41

The Holy Spirit, therefore, is the Spirit of life in Christ Jesus, or in other words, is the holy *life* or *nature* of Christ, of which we are to be made partakers; as the Scripture expresses it, partakers of the divine nature.

What Is the Baptism?

This brings us to our second question as to what it is to be baptized with the Holy Ghost.

The word "baptize" means to immerse, to dip into. Baptism with anything, therefore, must mean being immersed, or dipped into, that thing. To be baptized with the Holy Ghost means to be immersed into the Spirit of God, as to character or nature.

It is variously described as participation in the divine nature (2 Peter 1:4), having Christ *dwell in your hearts through faith* (Ephesians 3:17), being a *temple of the living God* (2 Corinthians 6:16), being a *dwelling in which God lives by His Spirit* (Ephesians 2:22). To be filled with the Holy Ghost, therefore, means simply to be filled with God.

When we say of a man that he is baptized with the Spirit of Christ, we ought to mean that he is permeated by the divine Spirit and nature of Christ as the law of his continual being. The mistake is too often made of looking upon the baptism of the Spirit as an *experience* rather than a *life*; as an outpouring rather than an incoming; as an arbitrary bestowment rather than a necessary vitality. Yet the Scripture plainly teaches that the gift of the Holy Spirit is a universal gift to all believers, one without which they cannot be believers at all. It is impossible to be a child of God without the Spirit, for the new birth is distinctly declared to be a birth of the Spirit (John 3:5-6).

Everyone, therefore, who is born of God is born of the Spirit, and has the Spirit within him as his new indwelling life. *And if anyone does not have the Spirit of Christ, he does not belong to Christ* (Romans 8:9). The converse of this is necessarily true, that if any man belongs to Christ, he must have the Spirit of Christ.

In seeking the baptism of the Holy Spirit, therefore, it is not a new thing you are to ask for, but simply to recognize the presence of that which you already have, and to submit fully to His possession and His control.

Available and Free

The Holy Spirit is a gift, but the being baptized or filled with the Spirit is not a gift, but a command. Water is a gift, but the drinking of water is not a gift, but our duty. The sunlight is a gift, but letting the sunlight into our houses is our privilege and our duty. To be baptized with the sunlight is merely to get into it and let it shine, and to be baptized with the Spirit is the same.

In Acts 2:33, we are told that Christ *has received from the Father the promised Holy Spirit and has poured out* this promised gift upon the Church. And in Ephesians 5:18, we are commanded to *be filled with the Spirit*. The Holy Spirit is like the sunlight, which forces its way into every place where there is the slightest opening to receive it. The sunlight has been shed forth upon the world, and the Holy Ghost, the promise of the Father, has been shed forth upon the Church. Every man born into the world shares the world's sunlight, and may have as much or as little of it as he pleases, and every man born into the Church (I mean, of course, the invisible Church of all believers) shares the Church's gift of the Holy Ghost, and may have as little or as much as he pleases.

Available to All

In Acts 2:38-39, the Apostle Peter, in the very first sermon preached in this new dispensation, announced that whoever believed in Christ should receive the wonderful gift, declaring to the people in the plainest words that it was their inalienable birthright: *The promise is for you and your children and for all who are far off— for all whom the Lord our God will call.*

It was not to be a special gift to a few, but belonged universally to every awakened soul. Yet, in spite of all this, there were Christians then as now who did not receive this filling with the Spirit. Paul found such at Ephesus (Acts 19:1-2). These Christians were like many in the Church now. They had not so much as heard of their glorious possession of the Holy Ghost. The question was not, "Has God given?" but "Have you received?" Such Christians are like blind men, who do not know the sun is shining, and do not open their windows and let it in.

These blind believers in Jesus kneel down in their shut-up hearts and pray for the baptism of the Spirit, when all the while this longed-for Holy Ghost is beating upon every avenue of their being, seeking for an entrance.

There is, in the lives of many Christians, an experience of a wonderful and instantaneous baptism, which makes an epoch in their lives, and which seems to transform their characters. In the light of the above teaching, what is the explanation of this?

It is, as we have proved, an incontrovertible fact that every child of God is and must be indwelt by the Spirit of God. But it is equally a fact that not all are filled with this Spirit. The definite, conscious experience, of which so many speak as the baptism of the Holy Ghost, is simply the moment when the soul, either consciously or unconsciously surrenders itself fully to this divine incoming.

The command is, *Be filled with the Spirit,* and we obey this command by abandoning our whole selves to God, and opening every avenue of our being to His possession. Like sunlight or like the wind, He enters and fills every spot that is opened to Him. The result of this, when done suddenly, is often a very emotional and overwhelming sense of His presence. But this sudden experience does not rise from the fact that anything new has been shed forth from God, but only that which has been already shed forth on the day of Pentecost is now allowed to enter and take full possession.

It is not more of the Spirit the lifeless Christian needs, but only that the Spirit should have more of him. And the conscious baptism is not the coming of the Spirit as of a thing from the outside, but the full taking possession of the whole being by the Spirit already dwelling within. You have been sealed with the Holy Spirit of promise, but there are doors to be unlocked and rooms to be occupied before it can be truly said that you are filled with all the fullness of God.

Known by the Fruit

In seeking for the baptism of the Holy Ghost, it is not God's attitude towards us that needs to be changed, but our attitude towards Him. He is not to give us anything new, but we are to receive in a new and far fuller sense that which He has already given.

The vital importance of this teaching will be realized by all who have, either in their own experience, or in dealing with others, known something of the extreme difficulties connected with this subject. Earnest, devoted souls have been brought into great darkness because they have not realized in their own experiences the wonderful baptism of which others speak. They think they cannot have received the longed-for gift because their emotions and sensations have not been like those described by others. The fruit of the Spirit is manifested, often, to a great degree in their lives, but they are afraid to attribute this fruit to the indwelling power of the Holy Ghost for fear they may be claiming a blessing that they do not really possess.

Now if it were really true that no one has received the Spirit as an indwelling guest but those who have had some definite conscious experience of baptism at a certain clearly marked time, how are we to account for the fruit of the Spirit so beautifully developed in many devoted lives, who have known no such epoch in their experience? Is not a tree to be known by its fruit, and can any power but the Holy Spirit produce holiness of heart and life?

On the other hand, dare we characterize all the wild fanaticism or the many un-Christlike, self-seeking ways of some who have received a "wonderful baptism" as being the genuine fruit of that Spirit, whose essential characteristics are a Christlike wisdom and a Christlike spirit of meekness and self-sacrifice?

How Can I Be Filled?

How can I personally as a child of God come unto this baptism and be filled with the Spirit? As in every other experience in the divine life, the things necessary on our part are surrender and faith.

1. We must be convinced that it is a fact that we, as the children of God, are indwelt by the Spirit of God.

2. We must abandon ourselves wholly—body, soul, and spirit—for His full possession. We must throw wide open every chamber in our inward temple and let the Heavenly Guest enthrone Himself in all.

3. Then we must believe that He does take full possession, and that we are filled with the Spirit up to the measure of our capacity to receive, and we must begin from that time onward to reckon on His presence and power as a continual fact in our lives and experience.

4. We must hold here steadfastly, regardless of all appearances, going quietly forward in a life of simple obedience to the Spirit now enthroned within; and the result will be that very soon the fruit of the Spirit will manifest itself in a blessed abundance.

The entrance upon this life of full surrender to the control of the indwelling Holy Ghost may often bring a sudden and perhaps almost overwhelming flood of emotion. But in other cases it may come, as it were, without observation in a quiet gladness and confidence, with a continual increasing development of spiritual power.

But however this may be, the essential *facts* are as we have seen, and the soul's part is only and always to recognize the indwelling presence of the Holy Ghost, and to yield utterly to His control. For this is the baptism of the Holy Ghost.

"O may the seed they have received have its fruit unto holiness, and in the end everlasting life."

—John Wesley

What Is Christian Perfection?

by John Wesley

Christian perfection is the loving of God with all your heart, mind, soul, and strength. This implies that no wrong temper, no contrary love, remains in the soul, and that all the thoughts, words, and actions, are governed by pure love.

Q. Do you affirm that this perfection excludes all infirmities, ignorance, and mistake?

A. I continually affirm quite the contrary, and always have done so.

Q. But how can every thought, word, and work be governed by pure love, and the man be subject at the same time to ignorance and mistake?

A. I see not contradiction here: "A man may be filled with pure love, and still be liable to mistake." Indeed I do not expect to be freed from actual mistakes, till this mortal puts on immortality. I believe this to be a natural consequence of the soul's dwelling in flesh and blood. For we cannot now think at all, but by the mediation of these bodily organs which have suffered equally with the rest of our frame. And hence we cannot avoid sometimes thinking wrong, till this corruptible shall have put on incorruption.

The Bristol Conclusions

Q. What was the judgment of all our brethren who met at Bristol in August 1758, on this head?

A. It was expressed in these words. (1) Every one may mistake as long as he lives. (2) A mistake in opinion may occasion a mistake in practice. (3) Every such mistake is a transgression of the perfect law. Therefore, (4) every such mistake, were it not for the blood of atonement, would expose to eternal damnation. (5) It follows, that the most perfect have continual need of the merits of Christ, even for their actual transgressions, and may say for themselves, as well as for their brethren, "Forgive us our trespasses." This easily accounts for what might otherwise seem to be utterly unaccountable; namely, that those who are not offended when we speak of the highest degree of love, yet will not hear of living without sin. The reason is, they know all men are liable to mistake, and that is in practice as well as in judgment. But they do not know, or do not observe, that this is not sin, if love is the sole principle of action.

Dependence Is Not Negated

Q. But still, if they live without sin, is it not plain that they stand no longer in need of Christ in His priestly office?

A. Far from it. None feel their need of Christ like these; none so entirely depend upon Him. For Christ does not give life to the soul separate from, but in and with, Himself. Hence His words are equally true of all men, in whatsoever state of grace they are: "As the branch cannot bear fruit of itself, except it abide in the vine; no more can ye, except ye abide in Me." In every state, we need Christ in the following respects. (1) Whatever grace we receive, it is a free gift from Him. (2) We receive it as His purchase, merely in consideration of the price He paid. (3) We have this grace, not only from Christ, but in Him. For our perfection is not like that of a tree, which flourishes by the sap derived from its own root, but like that of a branch which, united to the vine, bears fruit; but, severed from it, is dried up and withered. (4) All our blessings—temporal, spiritual, and eternal—depend on His intercession for us, which is one branch of His priestly office, whereof therefore we have always equal need. (5) The best of men still need Christ in His priestly office to atone for their omissions, their shortcomings (as some not improperly speak), their mistakes in judgment and practice, and their defects of various kinds. For these are all deviations from the perfect law, and consequently need an atonement.

To explain myself a little further on this head: (1) Not only sin, properly so called (that is, a voluntary transgression of a known law) but sin, improperly so called (that is, an involuntary transgression of a divine law, known or unknown) needs the atoning blood. (2) I believe there is no such perfection in this life as excludes these involuntary transgressions which I apprehend to be naturally consequent on the ignorance and mistakes inseparable from mortality. (3) Therefore, sinless perfection is a phrase I never use, lest I should seem to contradict myself. (4) I believe a person filled with the love of God is still liable to these involuntary transgressions. (5) Such transgressions you may call sins, if you please: I do not.

Q. How shall we avoid setting perfection too high or too low?

A. By keeping to the Bible, and setting it just as high as the Scripture does. It is nothing higher and nothing lower than this—the loving of God with all our heart and soul, and our neighbor as ourselves. It is love governing the heart and life, running through all our tempers, words, and actions.

Progression in
Holiness

by Joseph H. Smith

Holiness is absolute only with God. Not until we who are redeemed have been made "pillars in the holy temple" above are we beyond the probationary perils of lapsing. Hence while God's own holiness is independent, infinite, and final, ours is dependent, finite, and progressive.

It follows, then, that the perfected holiness that we are eligible for here, and to which we are enjoined by Christ and His apostles, and urged and aided by the Holy Spirit, is that which involves constant pursuit and leads to continuous progression rather than consummation.

In the fourth chapter of Ephesians, perfection is pressed upon all believers in order that we may *become mature, attaining to the whole measure of the fullness of Christ.* In the Epistle of Jude, we are told to *build ourselves up in our most holy faith.* And in Philippians, chapter three, Paul the apostle presents his own example as the type for the perfect Christian, in that, like one stripped for a race, he is pressing toward the mark, to reach that for which he was apprehended of Christ. And when the Savior proffered perfection to the rich young ruler to meet his confessed need, it was that he might be qualified to follow Him and fulfill his calling, and lay up treasures in heaven.

Moreover, reading carefully in Romans 8:28-29, we shall see that the "good" to which all things work together for those who are called according to His purpose is that of being "conformed" to the image of His Son. Since this "working" of all things is continuous through life, it is evident that the transforming into His likeness is still taking place.

While there has been a perfect cleansing, there is still *in process* a polishing and refining. While there has been an elimination or cure of the weakness whereby, though willing, we were unable to

50

perform, there are still to be added accretions of the power of the Spirit of holiness so that we may do exploits in the Kingdom's service, and not only be made able to withstand in the evil day, but having done all, to stand. (See Ephesians 6:13.)

"Destructive" Holiness

We may submit, therefore, that the "perfecting of holiness," which is possible, is both destructive or eliminative, and equipping or endowing for the lifelong pursuit of and eternal progress in the holiness of God.

It is to qualify us for that paradoxical race which we *run with perserverance* that we *may share in His holiness* (Hebrews 12:1, 10), that we are rid of *the sin that so easily entangles* and divested of *everything that hinders.* And this divestment of what hinders for ascent, with this deliverance from *the sin that so easily entangles* constitutes the negative side of Christian perfection. It is freedom from what (within us or about us) prevents or obstructs our progress in the way of holiness. Sanctification is, first of all, an act of destruction rather than a work of construction.

"Constructive" Holiness

This is but one hemisphere of the present experience of holiness. There is another. This is decidedly positive. The Fall had not only *depraved* us, it *deprived* us. The leper is no more typical of the sinful state than the palsied man who had been carried by four, or the impotent man who could not get down to the troubled waters to be healed. Not only have we done the evil that we would not, but the good that we would, we found ourselves unable to perform.

Neither our desires, nor our resolution, nor our best efforts, nor all our mere human helps can advance us in the holiness of God. Not only is the summit altogether unattainable, but the altitudes to which we are called and for which we were made, surpass our possibility, except by power from on high. Not only for the service that is enjoined, and not only for the afflictions we are able to endure in the "school of suffering," but for the ever-progressing ascent into the love of God, we need to be strengthened with might by His Spirit in the inner man.

Hence the Pentecostal power room must complement the cleansing stream of Calvary, in order to perfect holiness. We need first to be rid of all unholiness and then to be possessed with the ever-flowing fountains of living waters, which, like "rivers flowing from us," both refresh the thirsty earth about us and bear us up by their tides into the very bosom of God.

I then earnestly exhorted the society to follow after peace and holiness.

We have all need of more love and holiness.

—John Wesley

What's in a Name?

by Robert W. McIntyre

What is the significance of the name *Wesleyan*? It is derived from the name of an 18th century clergyman of the Church of England, John Wesley. Wesley was God's chosen instrument to restore an emphasis on the truth that Christ calls His redeemed to lives of love and holiness.

At first, the term *holiness* might sound so strange in a secular world that one would think it had escaped from a cage behind stained glass windows and wandered into unfamiliar territory. Not so. For why do the media give space and time to the follies, foibles, and failures of religious personalities if not because we all have the ideal, if not the expectation, of a holy life? It is the surprise of the failure to meet this norm that makes the story newsworthy.

Consider These Observations

First, in a world of wickedness, holiness remains an ideal. There is no need to establish the case that society is flawed. The evidence is all around us. Yet the ideal of holiness exists not only in the Church, but also in society. Codes of ethics, investigations, indictments, convictions, and even the evaporation of political candidacies all testify to society's disappointment at finding a flaw in the ideal.

Second, in a world of mass movements, holiness is essentially personal. The return to monasticism featured in a recent issue of *Christianity Today* is an expression of this.

That this is a world of large-scale movements is obvious. Another term for it is *peer pressure.* The advertising writer who can start a fad has it made. A fad—that is, the popular notion that "everyone is doing it"—becomes the criterion for ethical judgments.

Whether it is drugs, alcohol or sexual immorality, the pressure comes from the crowd, but the decision reveals the coward.

Third, in a world of rampant individualism, holiness has a social dimension. The fact that we are social creatures is undeniable. Jesus, our model, *grew in wisdom and stature, and in favor with God and men* (Luke 2:52, emphasis added).

Holiness Is Social

That 18th century clergyman, from whom the word *Wesleyan* is derived, both preached and practiced the social dimension of holiness. Preaching on Christ's Sermon on the Mount, he said, "Christianity is essentially a social religion. To turn it into a solitary one is to destroy it" (*Wesley's Works,* Volume V, page 296). Wesley explains that this does not deny the need for personal communion. Meekness is an essential Christian attitude. But how can one be meek in a vacuum? Peacemaking is a Christian activity. But how can one make peace in a vacuum? "Solitary Christian" is little less than a contradiction in terms.

He then put feet to his preaching. Wesley was a social activist, but not in the way that the term is used today. He didn't organize a demonstration to persuade the government to look after the poor. He did it himself. In fact, in that cause, he spent all but a minimum of his own money and then raised funds from others.

"I want you to converse more, abundantly more, with the poorest of the people," Wesley exhorted his workers. "Do not confine your conversation to genteel and elegant people. I should like this as well as you do, but I cannot discover a precedent for it in the life of our Lord or any of his Apostles. My dear friend, let you and I walk as He walked" (*Wesley's Works,* Volume XII, page 301).

Holiness to All, from All

Social holiness must stem from a holy social conscience that first seeks to establish wholesome and constructive standards for society and then responds in a loving way to the needs of those less privileged. The model of the truly holy person is not the ascetic but the athlete. The model of the holy person is the one who is holy, not because of outer protection, but because of an inner Presence; who is part of the world like the elements in a stew, not like the homogeneity of the melting pot; who is not changed by it but reaches out to change it, whether one by one or many by many. What we must have now is holiness for the streets, alleys, and marketplaces of this world . . . holiness in tuxedos and holiness in overalls . . . holiness in white collars and holiness in blue collars and holiness in no collars at all.

An aged grandmother, who never attended school, once gave her granddaughter a slip of paper which contained all the advice she would ever need to live a good life. What she wrote is valuable for all of us: "Wash what is dirty. Water what is dry. Heal what is wounded. Warm what is cold. Guide what goes off the road. And love people who are the least lovable, because they need it most." That grandmother wrapped a life philosophy around the needs of the world much as Jesus did when He said, "Feed the hungry, give drink to the thirsty, visit the imprisoned, clothe the naked. . . . Freely you have received, freely give."

Holiness with personal implications and ramifications for social compassion: that is a significant part of what's in the name *Wesleyan*. The world still responds to practical social holiness. Christ has no feet and no hands but ours.

Experience

The Apostle Paul met Christ on the Damascus road. His encounter was with a person, not an idea. The experience left him changed. Isaiah had a vision of God. He saw the Holy One in His splendor. It was that event which empowered his ministry.

This is always true of holiness: it is experiential. And this experience of holiness, sanctification, is not primarily a dogma or creed. It is an event. And it is this event that gives rise to the doctrine of holiness, and not vice versa.

The worst possible fate for the holiness message is that it should become simply that: a message. For it is not mere doctrine, but rather that *which we have seen with our eyes, which we have looked at and our hands have touched—this we proclaim.*

There is the experience of sanctification. Is it yours?

Jesus, Lover of My Soul

Jesus, Lover of my soul,
let me to Thy bosom fly,
while the nearer waters roll,
while the tempest still is high!
Hide me, O my Savior, hide
till the storm of life is past.
Safe into the haven guide.
O receive my soul at last!

Plenteous grace with Thee is found,
grace to cover all my sin.
Let the healing streams abound;
make and keep me pure within.
Thou of life the fountain art;
freely let me take of Thee.
Spring Thou up within my heart;
rise to all eternity.

—Charles Wesley

This blessed life must not be looked upon in any sense as an attainment, but as an obtainment. We cannot earn it, we cannot climb up to it, we cannot win it; we can do nothing but ask for it and receive it. It is the gift of God in Christ Jesus. And where a thing is a gift, the only course left for a receiver is to take it and thank the giver.

—Hannah Whitall Smith

Questions and Answers about Sanctification

by Norman G. Wilson

What Does Sanctification Mean?

The New Testament Greek word for sanctification has two meanings. They are both given in any English dictionary you check. The first is to set apart to a sacred purpose or to religious use. In the Old Testament temple, for example, there were rooms that could not be entered by anyone but the priest, there were vessels and instruments dedicated for worship, and these were not to be used for common purpose. So we are to be separated from the world order for God's use (John 17:16).

The second meaning is to free from sin, to purify. The Bible teaches that we are not only to do good works, but we are actually to be good, cleansed, purified, and made free from sin. That cannot be done by good works, sincere effort, or a strong will power. The sin nature must be cleansed. Jesus died to accomplish our cleansing (Titus 2:11-14).

Is Sanctification Progressive or Instantaneous?

It is both. There is the progressive work of sanctification, which begins when you are saved. From that moment on, as you walk in obedience to God and His Word, you daily grow in grace. You become more perfect in your obedience and more closely conformed to the image of Christ (Ephesians 4:13).

There is also a crisis of entire sanctification when you present yourself totally (without any reserve clauses) to God. On your part, this is called total commitment or consecration. The baptism of the Holy Spirit will cleanse your heart from all inbred sin (Acts 15:9).

This is followed by a lifelong growth in grace as you develop a life of godliness and true holiness by faith in the cleansing, sanctifying blood of Jesus Christ (Colossians 2:6).

Is Sanctification Required or Optional?

It is an absolute requirement. It is the will of God that you be sanctified (1 Thessalonians 4:3). It is the reason Jesus died: *And so Jesus also suffered outside the city gate to make the people holy through His own blood* (Hebrews 13:12).

Didn't I Receive the Holy Spirit When I Was Saved?

Yes. No one can be saved apart from the Holy Spirit (John 3:5). But the fullness of the Spirit, or the baptism of the Holy Spirit, comes after you have been saved when you have made a complete sacrifice of your all to God (Acts 19:2).

Why Must I Be Saved Before I Can Be Entirely Sanctified?

That is because until you are saved, you cannot present yourself as a living sacrifice to God (Romans 12:1). You are dead in trespasses and sins (Ephesians 2:1). Only after you have been made alive can you commit your life to God.

Do I Need to Speak in Unknown Tongues as Evidence that I Have Received the Baptism of the Holy Spirit?

No. The Scriptures teach that the evidence of the fullness of the Holy Spirit is *fruit* not *gifts*. According to 1 Corinthians 13, it is possible to demonstrate the gifts and not have the Spirit. But the fruit of the Spirit is love, joy, peace, and so on (Galatians 5:22).

Can a Sanctified Person Be Tempted to Sin?

Yes. There is no state of grace that removes the possibility of temptation. Even our Lord was tempted in all points like we are, yet He was without sin (Hebrews 4:15).

Can a Sanctified Person Sin?

Yes. Sin is always a possibility. *So, if you think you are standing firm, be careful that you don't fall!* (1 Corinthians 10:12).

Is It Possible to Live a Holy Life Without Sin?

Yes. A Christian does not continue the habit and practice of willful sin. The Apostle Paul asks, *Shall we go on sinning so that grace may increase?* He then answers his own question. *By no means! We died to sin; how can we live in it any longer?* (Romans 6:1, 2).

What Happens if a Sanctified Person Sins?

You must confess that sin and receive the cleansing of the blood of Jesus (1 John 2:1, 2).

What Must I Do to Be Sanctified?

First, be sure your past sins are confessed and forgiven, and that you are walking in obedience to the light of God's Word. Next, recognize that you need to be sanctified, that it is God's will for your life, and that He is waiting to do it now. Then, commit every area of your life to the will of God. Also, pray in faith, asking God to give you the fullness of His Holy Spirit. *How much more will your Father in heaven give the Holy Spirit to those who ask Him!* (Luke 11:13). Finally, believe that God has kept His word and has done the work.

Pray Something Like This

Lord, You said in Your word that the will of God is for me to be sanctified. I recognize that need in my life. I offer You all that I am and ever will be, all that I have or ever will have. I surrender every area of my life to Your absolute control. Fill me with Your Holy Spirit; cleanse my heart and give me power to live a victorious, holy life. I pray in Jesus' name with thanks. Amen.

Called to Imitate God

by David Holdren

A serious reading of both the Old and New Testaments reveals that God is calling people to a holy life. The term "holy" most basically refers to God (Isaiah 41:14). A.W. Tozer puts it this way: "Holy is the way God is. He does not conform to a standard. He *is* that standard" (*The Knowledge of the Holy,* p. 112). Holiness speaks about Godlikeness or Christlikeness.

One of the most fundamental and descriptive calls to holiness is this: Be imitators of God, therefore, as dearly beloved children, and live a life of love, just as Christ loved us and gave Himself up for us as a fragrant offering and sacrifice to God (Ephesians 5:1, 2). In Scripture, there is no call to holiness that surpasses that one. All other Scripture relating to Christian character either echoes or describes that same call.

Begin

But how are we to be "imitators of God"? Where do we begin such a pilgrimage? Our call and conversion to salvation in Christ is a necessary matter. Essentially, when one is truly born again, it is literally a "turning around." It is a turning toward God, away from a life of separation from God. We are new creations in Christ.

Why? Because we have a new standing with God, a new future with God, and we have chosen to see things from God's point of view through personal acceptance of, and identification with, Jesus Christ. This turning to God results in a totally new direction, but it is not complete in development.

Learn

Since holiness means, fundamentally, being an imitator of God, a great deal depends upon our knowledge of the Holy One. We can only imitate as much of God as we know about Him. Thus, we see the importance of Jesus Christ, our example, Who says, *Anyone who has seen Me has seen the Father* (John 14:9).

Jesus gives us an understanding of God by word and example. And as A. W. Tozer reminds us, "Only the Spirit of the Holy One can impart to the human spirit the knowledge of the holy" (*Ibid,* p. 111).

It is, then, with careful design, that Jesus refers to the Holy Spirit of God as the "Spirit of truth." And it is of great importance that He prayed for the Father to sanctify us through the truth (John 17:17).

Jesus emphasizes to us that the Holy Spirit *will teach you all things and will remind you of everything I have said to you* (John 14:26), and that *when He, the Spirit of truth, comes, He will guide you into all truth* (John 16:13).

To what manner of life is an imitator of Christ called? God is love, and we are called to be imitators of Him. We are called to a life of pure, powerful, practical, and practiced love. Christ tells us that all the law and prophets hinge on the command to *love the Lord your God with all your heart and with all your soul and with all your mind . . .* and *your neighbor as yourself* (Matthew 22:37, 39). It is the call of highest magnitude and is stated in both the Old and New Testaments.

In the Epistle of 1 John, love is considered to be the basic test of discipleship (1 John 3:11-18; 4:7-12). Observe that, when Christ informs us that we should be perfect as the Father in heaven is perfect (Matthew 5:48), the context is love. Also be reminded that we are called to *live a life of love, just as Christ loved us and gave Himself up for us as a fragrant offering and sacrifice to God* (Ephesians 5:2).

Continue

As one seriously begins to pursue the life of holiness, of Christlikeness, or of full discipleship, it will be a humbling experience indeed. As we study the Scriptures, see more of the nature of God, and seek to be His true servants, we see how great the contrast is between our Savior and ourselves. The more we long to be like Him, the more we see how far we have fallen in sin from His likeness.

This often brings a person to a dilemma: the desire to imitate Christ is discouraged by the inadequacy to do so. (See Romans 7.) In that intimate struggle of the soul, however, God makes us aware of our need for total trust in His sufficiency and of our need to be obedient to Him.

St. Paul expresses his awareness of God's sufficiency when he urges us to offer ourselves *as living sacrifices, holy and pleasing to God* (Romans 12:1). We often describe this as a total surrender or consecration of ourselves to God. We offer ourselves as a vessel to be separated for God, cleansed and totally available to Him. It is a dramatic return of the clay pot to the creative Potter.

We become living sacrifices instead of limp or lazy ones. We are instructed:

> *Prepare your minds for action; be self-controlled; set your hope fully on the grace to be given you when Jesus Christ is revealed. As obedient children, do not conform to the evil desires you had when you lived in ignorance. But just as He Who called you is holy, so be holy in all you do; for as it is written: "Be holy, because I am holy"* (1 Peter 1:13-16; Leviticus 19:2)

Fully Surrender

This monumental and total surrender of oneself is very important. As forgiven, consecrated, and obedient vessels, we are pure and clean in God's sight, through Christ. But purity is not the equivalent of holiness. A pure vessel may be cleansed from sin and consecrated to Christ, but the pursuit of one called to holiness is to be *filled to the measure of all the fullness of God* (Ephesians 3:19), and to *become mature, attaining to the whole measure of the fullness of Christ* (Ephesians 4:13). Absence of condemnation and of all ungodliness must be built upon by adding the character and presence of godliness.

Holiness means doing all that we know to do to "let God be God" in our lives. The Holy Spirit of God, the Holy Scriptures from God, and the example of Jesus Christ must be our necessary sources of guidance, strength, and deliverance.

When we are as fully responsive to God as we know how to be in faith, consecration, obedience, and steadfastness, then we can live with a sense of assurance, security, and peace with God—and we can pursue peace with all men and the holiness without which no one will see God (Hebrews 12:14).

The Secret of Victorious Living

by O. D. Emery

She was possibly 28 years old. There was a vivaciousness about her as she said, "Pray that I'll make it this time." With those words, she turned and walked away.

It was at the close of a service where I had spoken on the subject, "How to Know the Will of God." She was one among several persons who had responded to an invitation for prayer at the church altar. Others had assisted in prayer for her. Finally, I was able to get to her, after praying for others. Now, ready to depart the place of prayer, she extended her hand cheerfully to greet me. Then, having spoken those words, she started away.

"Wait," I requested, "Let me ask you what you mean." She returned and rehearsed a story of repeated struggles in her Christian life. The lapses had been so frequent that she had begun to accept her status as normal. "I suppose I'm one of those people who is destined to be always up and down in my relationship with God," she said.

Something Better

I probably surprised her, but I replied, "Your Christian life doesn't have to be that way!" Immediately I could tell I had touched a sensitive emotional nerve. Tears came to her eyes, and she bowed again at the altar saying, "If that's true, then I've got to know the secret."

We prayed briefly again, but we talked at length. I opened my Bible to Galatians 5, and explained Paul's instructions to "walk in the Spirit," to "be led of the Spirit," and to "live in the Spirit." The principles shared with her are crucial to perpetuating the walk with the Lord, and I want to give them here. Perhaps someone else may be helped by them.

1. From the time we come to Christ for forgiveness of our sins, the Holy Spirit begins to seek the full surrender of our will. His persistence is aimed at conforming us to the likeness of Christ. Until He gains our "absolute surrender," as Andrew Murray termed it, the Holy Spirit cannot enter all areas of our lives.

2. When we reach the crisis point of surrendering our will, the Holy Spirit fully possesses us, and we are indeed "Spirit-filled." Now He is able to empower us for the glory of Christ. In that moment we are "more than conquerors" through Christ. Now the issue becomes how to perpetuate this victory.

3. The Holy Spirit is certainly more concerned about our continuing victory than we are. He creates within us a hunger for the Word of God and a thirst for communion with Christ. These appetites draw us to the times and places for the Holy Spirit to anoint us with Himself. These frequent anointings or refreshings are the essence of "walking in the Spirit," being "led by the Spirit," and "living in the Spirit," which Paul urges us to pursue in Galatians 5.

4. Those to whom Paul addresses his Galatian Epistle had flipped and flopped also between reliance upon grace and the law—between life in the Spirit and in the flesh. But Paul taught them a better way, a way to victoriously live in Christ by the Holy Spirit's controlling presence.

Surrender

At the close of our lengthy conversation, the young lady prayed a sincere prayer of surrender. She acknowledged to God that she had resisted the Holy Spirit's tender bidding many times. Surrendering, she now found the joy of being Spirit-filled, and she left that day with the affirmation, *I have been crucified with Christ and I no longer live, but Christ lives in me* (Galatians 2:20).

This is the secret of victorious living!

Godly Living in an Ungodly World

by David Vardaman

A nthony Roberts is glad to be alive. At first, Roberts claimed that he was shot through the skull with an arrow, while walking through a park in Grants Pass, Oregon. He later admitted that a friend was trying to knock a one-gallon gasoline can off his head. It was part of an initiation into a rafting and outdoor group called Mountain Men Anonymous. It cost him an eye, but doctors say it could have cost his life.

If sin exacted its price as instantly as this, there might be a sharp increase in holiness. But sin, like cholesterol, appears to be harmless, even while setting us up for catastrophic failure. One sausage patty won't cause a heart attack. It may trigger indigestion, but an antacid will neutralize that. So we have a second sausage biscuit. Then, after the fats have accumulated silently for years, they strike without warning.

James wrote, *Religion that God our Father accepts as pure and faultless is this: to look after orphans and widows in their distress and to keep oneself from being polluted by the world* (James 1:27). Peter instructs us to *make every effort to be found spotless, blameless and at peace with Him* (2 Peter 3:14).

How can we keep ourselves spotless, blameless, and at peace with Him?

Consecration

First, consecrate yourself to God. Give yourself to Him without reservation. Don't give only your sins to Him. Give all of yourself to Him—your unique personality, your talent, potential, spiritual gifts, creativity, imagination—everything that He put into you. *Offer your bodies as living sacrifices, holy and pleasing to God—this is your spiritual act of worship. Do not conform any longer to the pattern of this world, but be transformed by the renewing of your mind* (Romans 12:1-2).

Sanctification

Next, be sanctified. In John 17, Jesus prays for the disciples, saying, *My prayer is not that You take them out of the world but that You protect them from the evil one. They are not of the world, even as I am not of it. Sanctify them by the truth; Your Word is truth.* Sanctification is something like a cholesterol clean-out. Through sanctification, God cleanses our hearts from sin, taking away not only the eternal effects of sin, but also our taste for willful disobedience.

Scripture

Also, read God's Word every day. While the Holy Spirit does the sanctifying, God's Word informs us of the possibility of this deeper work of faith. The Bible is God's message to us. Read it daily for a lifetime. It will never lose its freshness. Like a literary classic, it reveals new meaning with each reading. Unlike classic literature, *All scripture is God-breathed and is useful for teaching, rebuking, correcting and training in righteousness, so that the man of God may be thoroughly equipped for every good work* (2 Timothy 3:16-17).

Avoid Sin

Just say no to obvious sin. Some sins are so basic, so obvious, that anyone can spot them. Check the Ten Commandments (Exodus 20). If God says don't do it, then don't do it. It's that simple.

Love One Another

Live by the law of love. The greatest commandment, according to Jesus, is to *Love the Lord your God with all your heart and with all of your soul and with all your mind and with all your strength* and *love your neighbor as yourself* (Mark 12:30, 31). When your heart prompts you to do an act of kindness and love, do it. Judge your thoughts and attitudes by the law of love. Ask yourself whether or not this is the loving thing to do, say, or think.

Anthony Roberts fell in with bad companions. By not exercising good judgment, he allowed himself to be placed in a life-threatening situation. One wonders whether he thought at all. By contrast, the Old Testament hero, Daniel, lived in a pagan culture, yet lived a righteous life. His life declares that even if we live *among* pagans, we needn't live *like* them.

There is a joy that is deeper than human suffering, higher than the clouds, wider than the conflict, stronger than all opposing forces, stronger than all conditions. It comes from the heart of God. It is the joy of the Lord. It cannot be strangled by the enemy, nor crushed by the power of darkness. Its voice cannot be stilled by the tumult, nor swallowed up by the raging of the tempest. It is deeper, and higher, and sweeter than all, saying, "My beloved, I am with thee to keep thee In all thy ways." This is holiness.

—P.F. Bresee

Holiness for a New Millennium

by John N. Oswalt

Holiness is a word that has fallen on hard times. We think of Bible-waving "holy rollers" or storefront churches with names like "The Sanctified Church of God of the Holiness Brethren." Or we think of prim, self-righteous people whose religion is defined by what they don't do.

That is not what biblical holiness is all about. Like many of the other great ideas of the Bible, holiness has often suffered mistreatment at the hands of its greatest friends. But because an idea has been mistreated, even abused, there's no reason to abandon it—especially if it is as near the heart of biblical religion as holiness is. Instead, we must find ways to recapture this essential truth and make it livable for our day.

Sharing God's Character

What is the essential truth of holiness? It is that God's purpose for us is to share His character. In many ways, Christian teaching has lost sight of this. We have taught ourselves that God wants us to be happy, free from guilt, well adjusted, saved from eternal condemnation, open-minded and materially blessed. It's a problem rooted in the way we have handled the dearest of all evangelical doctrines: salvation by grace alone. The Bible is crystal clear on this point. None of us can make ourselves acceptable to God by our own goodness. That is the way of human pride, and human pride is the essence of sin.

Transformation

You may have seen a bumper sticker that says, "Christians aren't perfect, just forgiven." According to many, the purpose of the Christian religion is to get—to get forgiveness and the happiness which flows from that forgiven condition. In effect, Christians have said, "Don't expect much from me in the way of character; it's only being forgiven that counts." But forgiveness is not the main point. Christianity is not about what we get from God in return for our religious behavior. Christianity is about the transformation of our character into the likeness of God's character. When Jesus' disciples were commenting on the rigorous righteousness of the Pharisees, He commented that the disciples' righteousness would have to exceed that of the Pharisees if they hoped to see the kingdom of heaven. The Pharisees' problem was not that they were not righteous enough. Forgiveness, or any of the other benefits we get from God, are not ends in themselves, but are means to a much greater end.

Delivered for Love's Sake

This is beautifully illustrated in the story of Exodus. Did God ask the Hebrew people to live perfectly righteous lives for a couple hundred years before He would deliver them from Egypt? Hardly! He delivered them for love's sake alone. It was only after they had been delivered and were on their way to the Promised Land that He offered His covenant to them. What were the terms? If the people would agree to belong exclusively to God, then He would care for them and bless them in wonderful ways. But what would it mean to belong exclusively to God? Would it involve strange rituals or secret magic? No. Apart from serving God alone, making no idols, not demeaning His reputation, and showing that all of their time was His by how they treated the seventh day, all of God's commands had to do with how they treated other people—ethics!

What does ethical behavior have to do with my relationship with God? Everything! In the covenant, God placed a series of ethical requirements upon the people. For example, they were not to oppress their workers. Then God said, "You must be holy, just as I am holy." God's holiness is not some magical essence. It is His *character*. Holy character is the goal of all God's covenants of love in the Old Testament.

The same is true in the New Testament. Over and over, Paul announces that anyone who thinks it's possible to make himself or herself good enough for God by keeping the Law (the covenant commands) is badly mistaken. Christ came to deliver us from bondage to sin and the Law! How could you even think of continuing to live in that bondage if you have ever experienced the love of God? (See Romans 6; Galatians 5 and 6; 1 Thessalonians 4 and 5.) Nor is this Paul's idea alone. It also appears in 1 Peter and 1 John. These apostles understood that God's purpose in delivering us from the condemnation of sin was holy living, mirroring the ethical character of God.

We Can Never Make Ourselves Holy

But there is a problem. Once you respond to God's grace with a desire to live His life, it would seem that all you have to do is live it. That's what the Hebrews thought. When Moses instructed the people to call down a curse of death upon themselves if they broke any covenant commands, they agreed at once (Exodus 24:18). Little did they know that within a month, they would be dancing around a golden calf! The rest of the Old Testament tells of the Jews' escalating despair over their inability to live the life of God, a life that they increasingly understood was the best life, the one we were all intended to live.

So, what do we do? One approach is to pad the biblical laws with additional laws, so that if one of these lesser laws is broken, at least the biblical laws are not. But, as Jesus pointed out in rather strong language to the Pharisees, that still does not get at the real problem—the heart. Our wills are not a clean page that we can give to God by a simple, decisive act. No, the Bible teaches that the human will is determined to serve itself, please itself, and exalt itself. It is only when we decide to accept God's love in Christ and attempt to live His life that we discover how deeply ingrained that twisted will is. Even righteous living can become just another attempt to make ourselves look good.

Power for Holy Living

God's plan confronted the problem from a completely different angle. His plan, as revealed in Scripture, was to give His Spirit. The human spirit was helpless to live a life of true holiness because it was held hostage by a perverted will. So God planned to give His Spirit to everyone. Until this point, the Holy Spirit had only been given to a few, select leaders. But now God's own Spirit would give people the power they needed to live out God's holy character.

God had promised through the prophet Ezekiel, *I will give you a new heart and put a new spirit in you; I will remove from you your heart of stone and give you a heart of flesh. And I will put My Spirit in you and move you to follow My decrees and be careful to keep My laws* (Ezekiel 36:26-27). This is why the disciples of Jesus were so excited when the Holy Spirit came on them. It was what the Hebrew people had been anticipating for hundreds of years—divine power to keep their covenant with God.

Many of us are like the couple who lived in an electrically-wired house and used candles for light. When asked why they didn't use the power, they replied that they never had the electricity turned on because they were afraid to let the power company know where they lived. They feared that somebody from the company would come and spy on them. The Holy Spirit is in us and is ready to fill us with Himself and empower us to be the holy people we were made to be. But often, we live in the dark. Our perverse wills hold us in slavery, telling us that if we really let the Holy Spirit take control, we will lose our independence. What we'd really lose would be our inability to live like Christ, our foolish pride and the self-centeredness that twists every good intention.

Biblical holiness is the freedom to live the life of God, even if everything around us is slipping into corruption, hatred and despair. It is not a life of self-righteousness, snobbery or bizarre, mindless behavior. It is loving God with all the heart, soul, mind and strength.

What You Need to Do

What do you need to do to experience God's holiness through the fullness of the Holy Spirit?

- Repent of your selfish determination to run your life the way you want.
- Believe that Christ really can give you His character, not just on the surface, but all the way through.
- Surrender your will completely to Him.
- Ask Him to fill you now, receiving His promise by faith.

This is the door to genuine holiness. Will you open it?

Samuel Logan Brengle

Holiness Evangelist

by V. Raymond Edman

A passenger train chugged out of a dusty station in the college town of Greencastle, Indiana, one summer's day in 1883. Aboard was a brilliant young orator who had every reason to believe that his skill would carry him to renown and eminence in his chosen career.

As the young man looked back at the receding figure of his friend and fellow graduate who had accompanied him to the train, he heard the shout, "I'd give a fortune if I could be as sure of being in the United States Senate as I am that you will be a bishop!"

The shouter on the station platform was A.J. Beveridge. He became one of the most influential U.S. Senators of his time. But he was wrong about his ambitious friend.

Samuel Logan Brengle forsook his study for the ministry to cast his lot with a new and strange religious movement, the Salvation Army, which was described by its founder as "moral scavengers, netting the very sewers."

Instead of becoming a bishop, Brengle became a quiet-spoken prophet to the poor. Instead of gaining a secure place of influence, he threw himself into the wandering life of an evangelist to society's dregs. Though he was accorded the Salvation Army's highest rank, next to that of general, he remained the humble apostle of holiness.

Shortly after his alma mater, DePauw University, conferred upon him the degree of Doctor of Divinity, he wrote in his diary, "Why, when I joined the Army, I thought they would almost want to blot my name off the alumni register!"

The event that so drastically changed the direction of Brengle's life occurred while he was studying theology. Though he had been converted as a boy in a little Methodist church in Illinois, his decision to become a minister was not the result of an unmistakable call to preach. Rather, he was keeping a promise he had made to God during his college days.

As the most brilliant public speaker of his fraternity, Delta Kappa Epsilon, he was sent to a national convention to speak on behalf of an important matter involving the status of his chapter. The burden of that responsibility weighed heavily upon him. The night before the crucial convention session, Brengle prayed, "O Lord, if You will help me to win this case, I will preach!" The next day, Brengle won the support of the convention. True to his word, he gave up the political ambitions he shared with his friend, Beveridge, and applied himself to prepare for the ministry.

So it was that in 1884, Brengle found himself at Boston Theological Seminary, having served briefly as a circuit preacher in Indiana.

Stirred by Moody's Preaching

Brengle was determined to become a great preacher. To that end, he sought the power of the Holy Spirit. "Surely a great preacher could do more for the glory of God than a mediocre one," he rationalized.

He had been deeply stirred by the simplicity and power of D.L. Moody's preaching. "If I can only be a great preacher like Moody!" he thought. "He ascribes his power to the baptism of the Holy Spirit. Perhaps if I seek this baptism, I shall have this power!"

For weeks, he searched the Scriptures. Then he began to examine his own heart. And what he saw there sickened him:

> I saw the humility of Jesus, and my pride; the meekness of Jesus, and my temper; the lowliness of Jesus and my ambition; the purity of Jesus, and my unclean heart; the faithfulness of Jesus, and the deceitfulness of my heart; the unselfishness of Jesus, and my selfishness; the trust and faith of Jesus, and my doubts and unbelief; the holiness of Jesus, and my unholiness. I got my eyes off everybody but Jesus and myself, and I came to loathe myself.

The first faint streaks of dawn on the morning of January 9, 1885, found Brengle at his study table. "Today," he told himself, "I must obtain—or be lost forever."

As he wrestled alone in his room, suddenly he saw the "I" smeared all over his aspirations to be a great preacher. He cried out, "Lord, if You will only sanctify me, I will take the meanest little appointment there is!"

Still, in the back of his mind was the thought, "Even if my following be small, I still can be an eloquent, powerful orator, building up my small section of the kingdom of God."

In a flash, he again saw the "I" standing in the way of his long sought-for blessing. Utterly broken, he prayed desperately, "Lord, I wanted to be an eloquent preacher, but if by stammering and stuttering I can bring greater glory to You than by eloquence, then let me stammer and stutter!"

Groping in Spiritual Darkness

"Let me stammer and stutter!" It was the final step in self-surrender. He fully expected the Spirit to clothe him with His presence. But nothing happened. His hands were empty, but his heart was still hungry.

Still seated at his desk, he groped in spiritual darkness. Where is the blessing? Suddenly, as from a hidden well, the words came to him: *If we confess our sin, He is faithful and just and will forgive us our sins and purify us from all unrighteousness.*

The words broke across his heart like a refreshing stream. Instantly the grace and faithfulness of God dawned upon him. As he dropped his head in his arms and murmured confidently, "Lord, I believe that," a great sense of peace flowed over him. His face registered what had happened. Twenty minutes later, a friend to whom he returned a borrowed book looked at him sharply and said, "Sam, what is the matter? You look so different!"

The next morning, he met, on the street, a man known as the Hallelujah Coachman. When Brengle told him of his experience, the unlettered man cried, "Brother Brengle, preach it!"

The next day, Sunday, Brengle did just that in the church where he was student pastor, taking as his text Hebrews 6:1: *Therefore let us leave the elementary teachings about Christ and go on to maturity.* Two days after this public testimony, Brengle experienced a yet fuller revelation of Holy Spirit power. He described it:

I awoke that morning hungering and thirsting just to live this life of fellowship with God, never again to sin in thought or word or deed against Him, with an unmeasurable desire to be a holy man, acceptable unto God. Getting out of bed about six o'clock with that desire, I opened my Bible and, while reading some of the words of Jesus, He gave me such a blessing as I never had dreamed a man could have this side of heaven. It was an unutterable revelation. It was a heaven of love that came into my heart. My soul melted like wax before fire. I sobbed and sobbed. I loathed myself that I had ever sinned against Him or doubted Him or lived for myself and not for His glory. Every ambition for self was now gone. The pure flame of love burned it like a blazing fire would burn a moth.

I walked out over Boston Commons before breakfast, weeping for joy and praising God. Oh, how I loved it! In that hour I knew Jesus, and I loved Him till it seemed my heart would break with love. I was filled with love for all His creatures. I heard the little sparrows chattering; I loved them. I saw a little worm wriggling across my path; I stepped over it; I didn't want to hurt any living thing. I loved the dogs, I loved the horses, I love the little urchins on the street, I loved the strangers who hurried past me, I loved the heathen—I loved the whole world!

Did the Experience Last?

Brengle wrote decades later: "I have never doubted this experience since. I have sometimes wondered whether I might not have lost it, but I have never doubted the experience any more than I could doubt that I have seen my mother, or looked at the sun, or had my breakfast. It is a living experience."

He fully realized, however, that the experience was only the beginning of the life inhabited by the Holy Spirit. He says:

In time God withdrew something of the tremendous emotional feelings. He taught me I had to live by my faith and not by my emotions. I walked in a blaze of glory for weeks, but the glory gradually subsided and He made me see that I must walk and run instead of mounting up with wings. He showed me that I must learn to trust Him, to have confidence in His unfailing love and devotion, regardless of how I felt.

At another time he indicated, "I have prayed for years that my light and my love might keep step with each other. Light without love may lead to pride—may make us supercilious and give us a false sense of superiority. Love without light may lead to great indiscretions and false judgments and fanaticism."

Brengle's biographer wrote: "Before sanctification, preaching meant honors for Brengle; now it was to mean glory for Christ. Hitherto preaching meant exaltation of self; now it would mean exaltation of a Savior from self. Previously he preached to please; now he would preach to disturb. Whereas his sermons made men say, 'How beautiful is his oratory!' hereafter they would cause men to exclaim, 'How black are my sins!'"

Not long after his mountaintop experience, he went to hear William Booth, dynamic founder and general of the Salvation Army. He was tremendously drawn to the man and his mission. Other contacts with the organization brought him to the realization, "these are my people." Brengle turned down the offer of the pastorate of a new and affluent church built by the millionaire wagon builder Clement Studebaker in South Bend, Indiana. Instead, in 1886, he journeyed to London to be trained as a Salvation Army officer.

No name is more revered among Salvationists today than that of Commissioner Samuel Logan Brengle. He was one of the Salvation Army's most effective evangelists and teachers of the higher spiritual life. For forty years he traveled the length and breadth of the United States with his message of salvation through the blood of the Savior, and fire by the indwelling presence of the Holy Spirit.

In later years, when thinking of the high aspirations of his college years, he said: "If I had thought when I was on my way to Boston that I was ever going to join a tatterdemalion Army of that kind, I probably would have dropped off the train at some river and drowned myself!"

Brengle couldn't know the kind of man he would become. But the Holy Spirit knew. And when Brengle fully yielded to Him, He molded him into the man God wanted him to be—just as He can do in the life of any completely surrendered child of God today.

Rediscovering the Holiness of God

by Steve DeNeff

Think of the attributes of God as spokes on a wheel. If followed long enough, each will take you back to the hub of His holiness. As spokes emanate from the hub, so the attributes of God emanate from His holiness, which brings them together in an orderly fashion. Yet most of us see only His attributes (love, justice, mercy, and goodness), and not His holiness.

Isaiah's Vision of God

That was the case in Israel. Who can forget Isaiah's vision of God in the Temple? (See Isaiah 6:1-8.) But what many ignore is the fact that this vision occurred during a time of great distress. Everyone was focused on Tiglath-Pileser, the mighty Assyrian king who was sweeping into Israel, gobbling one city after another (see 2 Kings 15:27). Jerusalem was buzzing. The people trembled. Who would keep the bloodthirsty Assyrians from ransacking the city? Isaiah's visit to the Temple was, quite possibly, associated with a national cry for God to save the city from destruction. The prayers of the day were for God's justice and faithfulness.

But in striking contrast to the events in Jerusalem, the scene in heaven was one of serenity. In the middle of this crisis, the angels were not throwing lightning to the earth. They were covering their faces and feet, worshiping God. They did so, not because nothing else mattered, but because nothing else mattered *more*. All of heaven was obsessed with the holiness of God.

Worship in Heaven

The same was true in the Revelation. God's throne was surrounded by lightning, thunder, and fire. But as the Apostle John passed through this hurricane of activity into its eye, he entered the calm yet compulsive worship of four living creatures. They cried, *Holy, holy, holy is the Lord God Almighty* (Revelation 4:8). Even as the earth disintegrated under plagues and wars, their worship continued. They were oblivious to everything else. The message is clear: The epicenter of heaven is the holiness of God.

Isaiah's rare insight had a stunning effect. The consequences of his visions and the sequence of them provide an outline for what happens when we rediscover the holiness of God.

He Is Exalted

First, where God's holiness is observed, the Lord is *high and exalted* (Isaiah 6:1). He ceases to be the private possession of a few people inside a certain denomination or era. He is bigger than life. This inspires real and spontaneous worship, as opposed to euphoria produced by music or mood. It maximizes our faith. We remember that *nothing is impossible with God* (Luke 1:37). It brings heroics back to our religion. The people of God enlist to help Him win the conflict with evil. All of this happens when the Lord is lifted up.

We Are Humbled

In the next moment, we are humbled. This is the second effect of God's holiness upon the watching saint. One of the peculiarities of Isaiah's account is that it took place *in the year that King Uzziah died* (Isaiah 6:1). It was common for prophets to date their calling by the year of a king's reign. Jeremiah, Daniel, Amos, Haggai, and Zechariah all did. But it was unusual to date it by the death of a king. Even more confusing is the fact that Uzziah wasn't even king when he died. Jotham was. So why would Isaiah associate his calling with Uzziah's death instead of Jotham's reign? It is because of the manner in which Uzziah died.

Second Chronicles tells the story of a sixteen-year-old boy who became king and succeeded beyond the measure of most who had come before him. He was rich, famous, and powerful. That was the problem. For, once he was king, Uzziah entered the Temple to burn incense on the golden altar. This was a privilege reserved for priests alone. As a result, he was struck with leprosy at that moment. But after being stricken with leprosy, he left the Temple and moved outside the city while his son, Jotham, reigned as king. In less than a year, Uzziah was dead and was buried by himself in his own gardens . . . a sad ending to an illustrious career.

As the prophet Isaiah stood in the Temple where Uzziah was cursed, he must have replayed the mental videos of that tragic day and remembered that the holiness of God is never to be trifled with. For it was here that God drew a memorable line of distinction between Himself and His creature. Isaiah would not have missed the point.

Each time we meditate on the holiness of God, each time He enters the room where we are worshiping, we are struck first with His greatness, and then with our own unworthiness. These experiences always go together, and should. "Genuine worshipers want to blot themselves out of the picture," wrote J.I. Packer, "so that all can concentrate, without distraction, on God alone." These people have learned they cannot exalt themselves and God at the same time.

We See Our Sinfulness

As the glory of God sucks the wind out of our self-inflated sails, we are smitten with a sense of our sinfulness. *Woe is me,* cried the prophet, *I am ruined.* He did not say, "I need a little help." Whenever we gaze into God's purity, we feel not only unworthy, but also sinful. The secret thought or passion that lurks in the dark caverns of our souls, the heart that no man can know, is suddenly exposed to a blinding light.

Genuine repentance is not the product of mood, fear, or guilt for having broken a faceless law. It is produced by remorse for having offended the Holy One who stands behind the Law. A spiritual brokenness, a keen sense of total depravity, cannot be taught or given away. It must be discovered, one convert at a time. So the revival for which the Church has prayed is not dependent on anything we can muster, but on whether or not we rediscover the holiness of God.

We Inherit Grace and Forgiveness

Those who have grasped the holiness of God inherit grace and forgiveness. These are the last things one would expect. Yet they are God's first response. But the sequence is critical. It was after the prophet repented that he was forgiven, not before. It was the very part of himself that he surrendered which the angel purified. One would expect a prophet who had just confessed to total ruin and uncleanness to feel worse than anyone. But the opposite was true. Not only did he acknowledge his cleansing, but he also volunteered to serve God before the day was over. This is the final link in the miracle of Isaiah's Temple-day. We should remember it well: Once we are forgiven, we are called into service.

We Are Called into Service

We are called into service by the same vision which first humiliated us. This is the supreme irony. We have a natural aversion to God's holiness, which sends us into hiding. Yet, if we are willing to stare down the grim prospects, we are not ruined or ridiculed. We are accepted and invited to serve.

Again, the sequence is crucial. God's holiness must humble before it recruits. But our pattern in the last 40 years has been something else. During the Church Growth Movement, which began in the late 1960s, the emphasis of the Church shifted from repentance to recruitment. Instead of evangelizing those whom we had, we doubled our efforts to recruit even more. Soon after, we developed an emphasis on the discovery and implementation of spiritual gifts.

It is easy to see where this has taken us. We have recruited, mobilized, and elected into power thousands of people who were never truly converted in the first place. The prospects of confronting them now with the authenticity of their conversion are slim. Our recruits are deep in the quagmire of hollow performance. Read again Isaiah 6:1-8.

In the year that King Uzziah died, I saw the Lord seated on a throne, high and exalted, and the train of His robe filled the temple. Above Him were seraphs, each with six wings: With two wings they covered their faces, with two they covered their feet, and with two they were flying. And they were calling to one another, "Holy, holy, holy is the LORD Almighty; the whole earth is full of His glory." At the sound of their voices the doorposts and thresholds shook and the temple was filled with smoke. "Woe to me!" I cried, "I am ruined! For I am a man of unclean lips, and I live among a people of unclean lips, and my eyes have seen the King, the Lord Almighty." Then one of the seraphs flew to me with a live coal in his hand, which he had taken with tongs from the altar. With it he touched my mouth and said, "See, this has touched your lips, your guilt is taken away and your sin atoned for." Then I heard the voice of the Lord saying, "Whom shall I send? And who will go for us?" And I said, "Here am I. Send me!"

First, we catch a new vision of God's holiness and our own unworthiness (vv. 1-3); then, we are smitten with a sense of our own sinfulness (v. 5); then, God forgives and converts us (vv. 6-7); and finally, He drafts us into His service (v. 8). *Unless we are renewed in this order, we are better left alone!*

More than anything, the new believer, the dying church, the fence-sitter, the political piranha, and the discouraged minister need an unveiled look at the holiness of God. It is not a cure-all. But it is the best prescription that we have.

Unconditional Surrender

by J. D. Abbott

Some of us can clearly remember the attack by Japanese forces on Pearl Harbor. There followed some astounding victories for Japan. Her troops occupied Manila, Corregidor, and Singapore, and other territory was overrun and claimed by her troops. The tide turned, however, on the Island of Midway and on Guadalcanal in the Solomon Islands. Japan's Prime Minister Tojo, whose popularity in the days of victory had soared until he styled himself in the manner of a fascist leader, then suffered the loss of the confidence of the people. His cabinet was replaced by another. After about ten years of bloody engagements, it was evident that Japan was losing the war. The Allies began to talk of "unconditional surrender." But battles were waged while peace talks were held at Potsdam. On the sixth and ninth days of August 1945, atomic bombs took their tolls on Hiroshima and Nagasaki. Those experiences will long be etched in our memories. The proud nation of Japan was humbled, and the emperor announced their surrender to the Allied Forces.

Surrender

On September 2, 1945, in Tokyo Bay, aboard the U.S.S. *Missouri*, representatives of the Japanese people signed "The Unconditional Surrender of all Japanese Forces," which was demanded by the Potsdam declaration. Thus ended the terrible events which had cost Japan the loss of a million and a half people and brought her to her knees in absolute surrender.

The kind of military and political surrender required of the nation of Japan during World War II is not strange in the annals of history. Remember the unconditional surrender of the Confederate forces under General Robert E. Lee at Appomattox Court House, which ended the American Civil War on April 9, 1865?

Also, on May 8, 1945, the German High Command surrendered unconditionally to the Allied governments, and the Allies "assumed supreme authority in respect to Germany, including all the powers possessed by the German government, the High Command, and any state, municipal, or local government or authority."

In war, surrender usually specifies several things, such as the precise moment when hostilities shall cease, the fate of the persons surrendered, the disposition of arms, the evacuation of territory, the care of the sick and wounded, and the taking over of civil government. Unconditional surrender terminates the war and entitles the victor to deal with the enemy's territory as subjugated and capable of annexation.

History has recorded that Ulysses S. Grant, on February 16, 1862, sent a message to General Simon B. Buckner that said, "No terms except an unconditional and immediate surrender can be accepted."

Submission

This is not totally different from the admonition of James, the brother of our Lord, who, in writing to the Jewish Christians, told them to submit themselves to God (James 4:7). Adam Clarke commented on that admonition with these words, "Continue to bow to all His decisions, and to all His dispensations."

When one unconditionally surrenders to the Lord, he subscribes to the admonition of Paul, which is found in the doctrinal epistle to the Romans (14:8) where he states, *If we live, we live to the Lord; and if we die, we die to the Lord. So, whether we live or die, we belong to the Lord.* Alford comments as follows: "We are, under all circumstances, living or dying (eating or abstaining, observing days or not observing them) Christ's: His property."

The directive of Deuteronomy 6:5 and its repetition in Luke 10:27 are clear enunciations of the unconditional claim that God has on us—*Love the Lord your God with all your heart and with all your soul and with all your strength and with all your mind.*

T. Brooks, writing on the subject of absolute self-surrender, said, "He that dedicates himself to God, dedicates all; he that doth not dedicate himself, dedicates nothing at all." What Aeschinus said to Socrates is what a Christian must say to God: "Others give Thee gold, silver, jewels, but I give Thee myself." Ah, Lord! There are some that give You their lips, but I give You my heart. Others give You good words, but I give You the best of my affections. Others give You a few cold prayers, but I give You my whole soul, for You are worthy; You alone are worthy. What the King of Israel once said to the King of Syria, "I am yours and all that I have," is what a Christian must say to Christ—"I am Yours, O Lord, and all that I have."

This blessed life must not be looked upon in any sense as an attainment, but as a obtainment. We cannot earn it, we cannot climb up to it, we cannot win it; we can do nothing but ask for it and receive it. It is the gift of God in Christ Jesus. And where a thing is a gift, the only course left for the receiver is to take it and thank the giver.

—Hannah Whitall Smith

Two Sides of Holiness

The Put Off, Put On Principle

by Joe W. Colaw

> *You were taught, with regard to your former way of life, to put off your old self, which is being corrupted by its deceitful desires; to be made new in the attitude of your minds; and to put on the new self, created to be like God in true righteousness and holiness* (Ephesians 4:22-24).

We all agree that the concept of living a holy life is a great idea. But how do we make it happen?

The typical three-point pattern for putting off the old self and putting on the new self is (1) I recognize a need for a change. There are some old things in my life I need to eliminate. (2) I pray and ask God to resolve the problem, counting on Him to change me. (3) I expect it to happen instantly and am often disappointed because it doesn't.

The problem with this method is that it is not complete. We usually draw the conclusion that the Spirit-filled life is not for us, and we continue to be frustrated Christians. What we need is to build an effective biblical pattern for putting off the old self and putting on the new.

The biblical pattern works something like this: Here is a truckload of soil dumped into a heap. Rain comes and rivulets trickle down the hill of dirt. After a considerable amount of rain has fallen, those rivulets become significant chasms. Our mental processes work in a similar fashion. We are taught to think in certain ways as we grow up. We watch the reactions of our parents. We tend to handle anger or other experiences the same way they were handled at home. The raindrops of our lives cut a pattern into our minds. When we become Christians, we are forgiven, but we still have lifestyles that need to be adjusted.

In Ephesians 4:17, Paul refers to the *futility of their thinking*. That futile thinking process is what needs to change. The lifestyle of a Christian will not change until the attitude of the mind is renewed. Otherwise, the same old pattern will continue.

We need to start the discipline process of renewing the mind. We may contend that we have certain genetic tendencies such as being grumpy or hot-tempered. If we continue to defend our weak areas, we have given Satan the ability to keep them as strongholds. The first step is to admit our need.

The acrostic ACTS helps us to Admit the need, Confess it as sin, Tell the Holy Spirit to take full control, and Start living the new life with a renewed thought and action plan.

Three things are vitally important if we are to start living this lifestyle.

The Alarm of the Holy Spirit

First, ask the Holy Spirit to set off the alarm in your conscience every time that trouble pattern begins to surface. Then learn to respond to that alarm.

I once saw a lady open her car door to put her groceries inside and the alarm system went off. Instead of deactivating the alarm, she got in and drove off with the alarm going! Can you imagine what her husband thought when she pulled into her driveway? She didn't know how to stop the alarm.

When the Holy Spirit sets off an alarm in us, we need to know how to shut off the alarm and move ahead in victory.

A Changed Mind

Second, we must saturate our mind and spirit with God's plan. We need to memorize Scripture, hiding it in our hearts so we will not sin (Psalm 119:11). We must start new, holy-living thought processes. When the alarm goes off, we must be ready with a plan for action. If the problem is anger, we need to have Scripture ready that helps us deal with that.

Fill your mind with positive things. Replace the old rivulets of thinking and renew your mind with God's Word. It takes more than just reading the Bible. The Word must be deeply embedded in our hearts so that it renews our minds and changes our attitudes and thinking processes. We need to respond in a godly, holy manner because we have His will and way in our transformed minds.

Yes, holiness means that the Holy Spirit comes in and takes control, but we must also start the discipline of renewing our minds by knowing and heeding God's Word.

Stay in the Word

Third, stay in the Word; never give up. Continue to develop new Holy Spirit-led thoughts by reading and applying the Word. Some of us have a tendency to be grumpy and bitter. We need to find out what God says about that attitude, returning to His Word continually and finding God's answer.

Paul did not consider that he had *already been made perfect.* He told the Philippians, *I press on toward the goal to win the prize for which God has called me heavenward in Christ Jesus.* He was continuing to learn a holy-living lifestyle and a renewing of his mind.

We have to keep pressing on. Mature Christians realize that they haven't arrived, and they keep pressing on and learning. This may bother some people, who think sanctification is a one-time experience. It is more than hitting an altar and making a full consecration. We do need to have a time and place where we completely surrender our soul and life to the Lord Jesus Christ. But it is just as certain that full surrender is marked by completely saturating the mind and spirit in God's Word. It's time to press on!

Advice to the Not Yet Perfect

by Clarence Bence

John Wesley was both evangelist and pastor. In his journals and sermons, we see a person of almost unlimited energy, who repeatedly calls his listeners to press forward to new levels of spiritual experience. He is not interested in a Christianity that only speaks of striving for impossible dreams and unattainable goals. Rather, he is confident that God does not command that which He does not expect to be achieved, or promise that which divine grace is unable to accomplish in the one who lives by faith. The final words of the *Plain Account* define the high limits of the Wesleyan doctrine of full salvation: "Now let me gain perfection's height."

Available Now

The present availability of perfecting grace through faith has been a recurrent theme in holiness preaching. In his sermon, "The Scripture Way of Salvation," Wesley summarizes the logic behind this immediacy of sanctification by telling his audience to "expect it by faith, expect it as you are, and expect it now." Since Christian perfection is not by works, there is no need to delay until some level of ethical purity is reached; one can be cleansed from the bent to sinning instantaneously in the present moment.

But what about the believer who hears the message of full salvation and yet cannot (for whatever reason) testify to the experience of entire sanctification? Followers of Wesley take his logic and go several steps further, suggesting that failure to enter the "promised rest" is purposeful defiance of God's will—a sin. Such a "sinner" not only is lacking in perfection, but might also be jeopardizing his or her very justification, since no sinner can expect to see God. Thus the term "holiness or hell" arises, suggesting to the unsanctified believer, no matter what point of spiritual maturity he or she has attained, that there are really only two options available to the *not yet perfect*—an immediate step of faith into the experience of heart cleansing or the gnawing fear that all salvation might be lost. Wesley's pastoral concern for his converts does not allow him to make such bold hints. Instead, he preached "Satan's Devices," a sermon that should be required reading for every holiness minister who would see his people come into a deeper relationship with Christ. One might expect that Wesley would counsel the unsanctified by pointing out all the temptations to carnality and sensual sin that the Devil uses to assault us. Instead, he suggests that the "grand device" of Satan is to draw attention to the spiritual perfection that has not yet been attained by the Christian and then to destroy what saving work has been done by the "expectation of that greater work" that seems so far from our grasp. Wesley says that "The more vehement desire we feel in our heart of the entire holiness He hath promised, the more we are tempted to think lightly of the present gifts of God, and to undervalue what we have already received, because of what we have not received."

Don't Despair

Wesley then proceeds to give detailed descriptions of how Satan attacks our peace, our joy, our faith, and finally our hope of ever being restored to the image of Christ. In despair of not attaining the goal, the Christian becomes fretful toward God for "thus delaying His coming," and envious of those whom He judges to have already attained the prize. Hence the strange irony—the very pursuit of holiness can become a detriment to those who are on the way.

Surprisingly, Wesley's response is *not* to push for immediate results. He exhorts the believer to hold fast to what he or she has already attained. The awareness of the sin that remains in one's life causes one to rely on the grace of God, "who hath done so great things for you already, and will do so much greater things than these." As to the delay in God's sanctifying work, Wesley offers this thought-provoking comment: "He cannot be straightened for time, wherein to work whatever remains to be done in your soul. And God's time is always the best time. Therefore be thou [fretful] for nothing."

While Wesley never directly addresses the concept of "holiness or hell," he comes close in his concluding words.

Thus, being filled with all peace and joy in believing, press on, in the peace and joy of faith, to the renewal of thy whole soul in the image of Him that created thee! Meanwhile, cry continually to God, that thou mayest see that prize of thy high calling, not as Satan represents it, in a horrid, dreadful shape, but in its genuine, native beauty; not as something that must be, or thou wilt go to hell, but as what may be, to lead thee to heaven. . . . In steadfast faith, in calm tranquility of spirit, in full assurance of hope, rejoicing evermore in what God hath done, press ye on unto perfection!

Thanks, Mr. Wesley! I needed that!

Theology without experience is like faith without works; it is dead. The energy of the flesh can run bazaars, organize amusements and raise millions of dollars; but it is the presence of the Holy Spirit that makes a temple of the living God.

—Samuel Chadwick

Effects

From darkness to light is a sweeping change. On the day that Thomas Edison was buried, electric lights across the country were dimmed in his honor. For a few moments the world became dark in tribute to the light bulb's inventor. In some sense we pay that same tribute with every flip of a switch. Electricity has had a dramatic effect upon our world.

Power is like that. What it touches, it will change.

As will holiness. The power of God released upon the human heart will move the switch from dark to light. *Love, joy, peace, patience, kindness, goodness, faithfulness, gentleness and self-control:* these are the effects of holiness. This perfect love we proclaim is not a one-time thing. It is a way of life that begins at the altar of consecration and continues through eternity. The sanctified life is a transformed life.

I Want A Principle Within

I want a principle within
of watchful, godly fear,
a sensibility of sin, a pain to feel it near.
Help me the first approach to feel
of pride or wrong desire,
to catch the wandering of my will,
and quench the kindling fire.

Almighty God of truth and love,
to me Thy power impart;
the burden from my soul remove,
the hardness from my heart.
O may the least omission pain
my reawakened soul,
and drive me to that grace again,
which makes the wounded whole. Amen

—Charles Wesley

Reflecting the Holiness of God

by Stan A. Toler

Do you remember the first time you heard your own voice recorded and played back? You probably reacted like so many others: "Do I really sound like that?" Or, have you ever had your picture taken and then remarked, "That doesn't look like me." Isaiah had a similar struggle with sight and sound.

> *In the year that King Uzziah died, I saw the Lord seated on a throne, high and exalted, and the train of His robe filled the temple. Above Him were seraphs, each with six wings: With two wings they covered their faces, with two they covered their feet, and with two they were flying. And they were calling to one another: "Holy, holy, holy is the Lord Almighty; the whole earth is full of His glory." At the sound of their voices the doorposts and thresholds shook and the temple was filled with smoke. "Woe to me!" I cried, "I am ruined! For I am a man of unclean lips, and live among a people of unclean lips, and my eyes have seen the King, the Lord Almighty"* (Isaiah 6:1-5).

Isaiah saw the holiness of God and heard the reaction of the adoring angels in His presence. Isaiah then looked at himself and said:

"That doesn't look like me."

"I don't sound like that."

I've seen some folks try to do it, but God's holiness is pretty hard to fake. They usually end up looking grim and joyless—like they've been baptized in embalming fluid. What an inaccurate reflection of God's holiness! And how out of tune that is with the seraphs that sang around His throne.

I'd rather be around the genuine article. C.S. Lewis said in *Letters to an American Lady*, "How little people know who think that holiness is dull. When one meets the real thing, it is irresistible." Isaiah gave us a glimpse of the wholly genuine *seated on a throne, high and exalted.*

Looking so out of place in God's presence, the prophet expresses an agonized longing to reflect what God truly is—holy.

The Image of Holiness

But what does holiness look like?

We have a problem in trying to describe holiness. We're like the Sunday school student who was asked to draw a Bible picture. "What's that?" her teacher asked after seeing the masterpiece. "That's God," the student quickly replied.

Concerned, her teacher commented, "Honey, none of us knows what God looks like."

Puzzled, the student replied, "Well, if we don't know what He looks like, then how can we be like Him?"

I'm glad that God solved the problem by giving us a glimpse of Himself in His Word—as much of a glimpse as we can stand this side of eternity. *For since the creation of the world God's invisible qualities—His eternal power and divine nature—have been clearly seen, being understood from what has been made, so that men are without excuse* (Romans 1:20).

In the Old Testament, He is seen in the awesome and unapproachable majesty of the throne, the burning bush, and the ark of the covenant. Later, in the New Testament, He is seen in the redemptive vulnerability of the manger cradle, the executioner's cross, and the borrowed grave.

Holiness characterizes God. And that holiness must be reflected in His people. *It is written: "Be holy, because I am holy"* (1 Peter 1:16).

It seems implausible. Reflecting God's holiness? Because of who He is, He could never be like us. But also because of who He is, He invites us to be like Him—as much as we can be, while living in the confines and confusions of planet earth. The impossible becomes possible through the provision of His Son, Jesus Christ, and the power of His Holy Spirit. Wesley said that the Holy Spirit is the "immediate cause of holiness."

The Reflection of Holiness

How, then, should we reflect God's holiness?

First, we do it through an unconditional hatred of sin. Proverbs 6:16-19: *There are six things the Lord hates, seven that are detestable to Him: haughty eyes, a lying tongue, hands that shed innocent blood, a heart that devises wicked schemes, feet that are quick to rush into evil, a false witness who pours out lies and a man who stirs up dissension among brothers.*

Reflecting God's holiness means rejecting sin. *No one who lives in Him keeps on sinning. No one who continues to sin has either seen Him or known Him* (1 John 3:6).

Second, we reflect God's holiness in an unconditional love for His people. *How great is the love the Father has lavished on us, that we should be called children of God* (1 John 3:1a). God's heart looks beyond the *deed* to the *doer*. He can't accept the sin, but He does wrap arms of acceptance and forgiveness around the repentant sinner.

As a boy attending camp meetings, I remember occasions following a stirring service when we would gather around a campfire for a time of praise and reflection. One by one, as other young people arrived, the circle was enlarged. Some of those who joined the circle weren't the holiest in disposition or conduct (at least before the service). But the presence of God, the warmth of the fire, and the glow on our hearts made a place for them in the circle.

Reflecting God's holiness means no closed circles. That doesn't mean approving of sin—in any form. It does mean having a heart that is inclusive rather than exclusive. In his message, "The Way of Holiness," Jonathan Edwards declares, "[Holiness] is sweet and ravishingly lovely."

Third, God's holiness is reflected in unconditional sacrifice for the welfare others. John 3:16 has been mocked by football fans, wrestling promoters, and stand-up comedians. But it will never be replaced as the definitive word on God's commitment to His creation. *For God so loved the world that He gave His one and only Son, that whoever believes in Him shall not perish but have eternal life.* He loved . . . He gave. He paid the ultimate price for the salvation of every person.

Reflecting God's holiness means the putting aside of self for the redemption of others. According to Paul the apostle, that selflessness is seen in the home as well as on the highways—Ephesians 5:25, *Husbands, love your wives, just as Christ loved the church and gave Himself up for her.* Chuck Colson said, "Holiness is the everyday business of every Christian."

Though we are not "little gods," as some religions teach, we can have a little of God in us. *It is because of Him that you are in Christ Jesus, who has become for us wisdom from God—that is, our righteousness, holiness and redemption* (1 Corinthians 1:30). A nineteenth-century Scottish theologian wrote, "Holiness consists in thinking as God thinks, and willing as God wills." And what is that? It is reflecting the holiness of God.

Sanctification is that work of God's grace by which we are renewed after the image of God, set apart for His service, and enabled to die unto sin and live unto righteousness. It comprehends all the graces of knowledge, faith, repentance, love, humility, zeal and patience, and the exercise of them toward God and man.

—Richard Watson

The More Excellent Way

by Thomas H. Hermiz

A lawyer approached Christ and asked, *Which is the greatest commandment in the law?*

Jesus replied, *"Love the Lord your God with all your heart and with all your soul and with all your mind." This is the first and greatest commandment. And the second is like it: "Love your neighbor as yourself." All the Law and the Prophets hang on these two commandments.*

The way of love, the more excellent way, is the way that leads to eternal life. Loving God with all of your heart and loving your neighbor as yourself are the basic essentials of the Christian life.

Loving God

What does it mean to love God with all our heart? In John 14:21, Jesus said, *Whoever has My commands and obeys them, he is the one who loves Me.* To love God is to have a passionate desire to obey and please Him. We must know His commands and, through the power of His Spirit, obey them. It is far easier to speak of love for God as some sort of emotional response to Him. The love God desires is love expressed in wholehearted, down-to-earth, day-by-day obedience.

You cannot love God with your whole heart in your own strength. The power and influence of sin are too great. The only way we can respond to this command is through the strength and grace of God. Through the power of His Holy Spirit, we can make a full surrender and keep His commandments.

Human nature is such that we must all have a master. God has given us complete freedom to choose whom we will serve. Some have enthroned their own egos. They live a selfish, self-centered life. Others worship another person or some philosophy. Some are totally enamored with their vocational ambitions. However, the

101

more excellent way, the way of love, is that which allows God to be the absolute Lord over every area of life.

There is a wonderful sense in which God makes it easy for us to love Him, by loving us first. He did something for us that no one else could do. *But God demonstrates His own love for us in this: While we were still sinners, Christ died for us.* When we consider the love, holiness, and fatherhood of God, it sets the sparks of love blazing within us.

The Apostle Paul gave himself to build the early Church. But as his life drew to a close, he could see only a string of tiny outposts along the Mediterranean, many of them weakened by immoral indulgences or divided over doctrinal issues. The very nature of the obedience that God demands is that it is given without regard to circumstances or results.

John tells us that if our love for God is complete, we will have confidence on the Day of Judgment. In 1 John 4:18, he declares that *perfect love drives out fear, because fear has to do with punishment.* Although perfect love will not free us from the phobias we have acquired throughout the course of our lifetime, it will set us free from the fear of the judgment and of the hereafter. The way of love is truly the more excellent way.

Loving Your Neighbor

You cannot separate loving God from loving others. This is another reason why the way of love is the more excellent way. It not only enables us to love God with all of our hearts, but it also gives us the power to love our neighbors as ourselves. In 1 John 4:20-21, we read, *If anyone says, "I love God," yet hates his brother, he is a liar. For anyone who does not love his brother, whom he has seen, cannot love God, whom he has not seen. And He has given us this command: Whoever loves God must also love his brother.* It is a complete contradiction to say we love God with all of our hearts and not love our neighbors as ourselves. Christian love never intentionally hurts or harms another person. It is a love that refuses to seek revenge. It declares that regardless of what anyone has said about me or done to me, I will never try to get even or to put that person down, but will always endeavor to lift him up. Christian love is a love that forgives and restores.

Loving Your Enemy

Christian love is more than an emotion. It is also an act of the will. It is a love that states, "I will turn the other cheek. I will go the second mile. I will forgive seventy times seven." This love is the fruit of the Spirit in the life of a Spirit-filled believer.

If we have the love of Christ in our hearts, we will be able to love not only those who love us and those who are lovable, but we will have the divine ability to love the unlovely and those who hate us. There is a desperate need in our world for this kind of love.

Our relationships with one another are a good indication of our relationship with Christ. To say we are in Christ, but to be out of fellowship with one another is a reflection on the name and cause of our Savior. One of the ways to draw closer to Christ is to draw closer to one another.

A dose of Christian love would heal many of the divisions and schisms within the church. I am concerned that we have preached this doctrine at a higher level than we have experienced it. Because of this, we have appeared to be phonies and hypocrites in the eyes of many.

If God has to bypass the holiness movement and raise up someone else to do the job that we have been called to do, it will not be because of our doctrine. We have a scriptural, sensible doctrine. Our problem has been that we have not always experienced and demonstrated true Christian love. Perfect love will enable us to rise above our differences and work together for the building of the Kingdom.

Another reason that perfect love is the more excellent way is that it delivers us from envy. Envy is the malignant feeling we have toward others because of their success or prosperity. It manifests itself in small ways, such as saying things that detract from the success of others, or by saying things that bring a cloud over their reputation.

Eric Honecker, who was the Marxist leader in East Germany for many years, was allowed to live in Russia when his country wanted him to stand trial for murders that he ordered. Mr. Honecker ordered his guards to shoot to kill anyone trying to get over the wall that divided East and West Germany.

Mrs. Honecker had been the Minister of Education for many years in East Germany. When Pastor Hugh Homer and his wife wanted to send each of their eight children to college, they were denied higher education by Mrs. Honecker simply because of their commitment to Christ.

When the Marxist government in West Germany crumbled, the Honeckers were left on the streets of East Berlin. No one, not even their Marxist friends, wanted to be identified with them. When Pastor Hugh Homer learned that the Honeckers were on the street, he invited them to stay in their home until they could make other arrangements. The Honeckers accepted the invitation and moved into the parsonage with the family that they had denied the privilege of higher education on eight occasions. After several days, Pastor Hugh Homer said that, although the Honeckers had not renounced their Marxist beliefs, they had begun to bow their heads and fold their hands when the family prayed around the dinner table.

This kind of love enables us to return good for evil, blessing for cursing, and love for hatred.

When Paul said, *Your attitude should be the same as that of Jesus Christ,* he was telling us that we could have the same disposition that Christ possessed. The life of Christ is characterized by oneness with the Father—perfect love for the Father and humanity, and a spirit of peace. When our hearts have been cleansed from all sin, and Christ is Lord, the atmosphere of our lives will not be one of strife and discord, but one characterized by love and peace.

The evidence is overwhelming that the way of love is the more excellent way.

Our Highest Priority

by Thomas E. Armiger

Max Lucado, writing in *Leadership Journal*, said, "Undefined priorities are at the root of much of our success-or-failure frustration." Setting priorities is a means of keeping the desires, demands, and duties of our lives in order. We constantly determine our priorities through a maze of options.

"What is important and what is less important?" we ask wisely. Assigning a priority to our tasks helps us decide on the most effective use of our time. If that is true personally and professionally, it is even more true for us spiritually.

What is our highest priority? Jesus defined it: *"Love the Lord your God with all your heart and with all your soul and with all your mind." This is the first and greatest commandment. And the second is like it: "Love your neighbor as yourself"* (Matthew 22:37-39). Notice that devotion takes precedence over duty.

The pursuit of holiness is the chief aim of God's people. No other purpose is more important than to have a heart that is totally His. Matthew 6:33a: *Seek first His kingdom and His righteousness.*

In light of that Kingdom principle, then, there are spiritual priorities that affect both our personal and our professional lives.

Worship Over Work

First, worship is more important than work. A.W. Tozer said, "God calls us first to be a worshiper, second to be a worker." It is far too easy to allow our diligent work for God to crowd out His work *in* us. Remember with me the familiar story of Mary and Martha as recorded in the gospel of Luke. Martha was so preoccupied with the preparations for Jesus' visit that she couldn't enjoy His presence. Jesus reminded her that her sister had chosen the more important—sitting at His feet in fellowship with Him. The Apostle Paul understood that priority when he declared: *I consider everything a loss compared to the surpassing greatness of knowing Christ Jesus my Lord, for whose sake I have lost all things. I consider them rubbish, that I may gain Christ* (Philippians 3:8).

Those who minister the gospel of Christ may know the facts about Him, and may have made a public commitment to preach and teach those facts. But their highest priority should be to know Him personally rather than just to know Him "professionally." There is no room in our churches for a third-person holiness. We cannot preach or teach something that we have not personally experienced. We cannot hope to take a message to the world that has not been birthed in our own conformity to the Word and will of God.

Character Over Calling

Second, character is more important than calling. The life of Moses illustrates the importance of a calling. Early on, he had a sense of purpose in leading the nation of Israel. But his calling became a higher priority than his conduct, as biblical history records. It resulted in the tragic death of an Egyptian, and Moses' forty years of obscurity.

God is still calling people to lead others to the Promised Land. But His leaders must be people of holy character. Holiness living is more important than holiness preaching, teaching, or administration. Paul advised Timothy to *set an example for the believers in speech, in life, in love, in faith and in purity* (1 Timothy 4:12b).

Anointing Over Activity

Third, anointing is more important than activity. Certainly we are called to be faithful stewards and to strive for personal excellence. But productivity should never be substituted for Pentecost power—a power that only comes in answer to prayer. Jesus said, *If you then, though you are evil, know how to give good gifts to your children, how much more will your Father in heaven give the Holy Spirit to those who ask Him* (Luke 11:13)!

Someone has said that prayer doesn't just help us with our work—*it is our work*. Prayer is a spiritual priority that we make every morning. It is an investment that pays dividends throughout the rest of the day. The Apostle said: *Neither he who plants nor he who waters is anything, but only God, who makes things grow* (1 Corinthians 3:7).

We must be productive. We must set worthy goals. We must calculate the cost and utilize effective methods for reaching our goals. But we must never forget that productivity alone doesn't make things happen—with any lasting results. It is God's *activity* in our *productivity* that produces eternal results.

The quality of our doing comes from the quality of our being. And the quality of our being comes from times of personal devotion—listening to, and obeying, God. It comes from pursuing God's holiness with all of our heart, soul, and mind. That is our highest priority.

Grace does not make men infallible. Sin has so perverted our moral and spiritual powers, that we shall never in this present life be free from the infirmities of human nature. Whatsoever our experience of the grace of God may be, the liability to error will cling to us until this mortal puts on immortality. Infirmities have their ground in our physical nature, aggravated by intellectual deficiencies. They are the outflow of our imperfect moral organization—the scars of sin which remain after the wound has been healed.

—Thomas Cook

The Power
of Holiness

by Bernard H. Phaup

The Word says, *You will receive power when the Holy Spirit comes on you.* The wind of Pentecost symbolizes force, energy, power. Paul said it like this: *For God did not give us a spirit of timidity, but a spirit of power, of love and of self-discipline.* This power may not be what some think. When the Holy Spirit comes, He brings purity and He also brings power. Yes, purity is power. The Holy Ghost is power. It is here that the weakness of the human is lost in the power of the divine.

Ability

A rather literal translation of Acts 1:8 could be as follows: *The Holy Ghost coming upon you, you shall be able.* Able for what? Able for anything that comes into one's life. Whether sacrifice, or suffering, or service, or self-denial, or cross-bearing, or labors abundant, or whatever God's will may be—you shall be able for it. How different it is when the divine ability takes over the human inability.

One must be seriously disturbed that in so many places there is such lukewarmness, such powerlessness, and such ineffectiveness. Certainly a part of the answer lies within this area of the power of the Holy Spirit coming upon us. Recall what happened in those early church days. Dare we believe that it could happen again in these days? There is no substitute for this divine force. When that is missing, then man programs too much. When that is missing, then churches frantically hurry about to seek a substitute. When that is missing, then organization becomes top-heavy.

If the Church is to meet the fearful onslaught of evil in this day, it can only be through the power of the Holy Ghost. May it please God to send upon His Church a renewal of Pentecost.

Passion

There is also passion associated with this truth. Pentecost carries with it a holy passion. One who has come to know Christ in saving grace will possess a burning passion to know Him better, and to have unbroken fellowship with Him. This will inevitably lead the obedient soul to the total commitment which results in the sanctified experience. Those who hunger and thirst after righteousness are the ones who are filled. The soul that is on a search for God will pant after Him as a thirsty person pants after the water brook.

This grace, possessing the heart, produces undying love and devotion. Life takes on a meaning and a sacredness that is unknown to those outside this circle of love. Then whether one preaches, or prays, or serves, he does so—not because of appointment or exaltation or because he is duty-bound—but because he is compelled by the inner fire, which burns as white heat in the soul. This kind of service does not stop to ask about conveniences, remuneration, or honor, but it is service for love's sake. It may even reach the point of holy recklessness to which Mary had come when she broke the alabaster box. To some it was waste, but to her Lord it was a fragrant and never-to-be-forgotten offering of love. Present-day preaching needs a new revelation of this passion, this burning heart.

It was said of one great preacher, "Passion, which is love on fire, burned within his soul and sent its warmth into the minds and hearts of those who heard him preach." It was said of Francis Asbury's preaching that, "He preached to the hearts of his hearers out of the heart of God." Another said of him, "He was a holiness preacher whose soul was aflame. Those who heard him saw the light and felt the heat of the impact of the Spirit's power upon him."

As Dr. Jowett expressed it, "We must bleed if we would bless." The fountains of hearts must be broken up if the dry and thirsty ground is to be watered. There must be a deep brokenness within the heart of the minister if he is to break stony hearts by divine truth.

Propagation

There must also be the propagation of this dynamic and wonderful truth. "All the defects, deflections, imperfections, and failures of the modern churches have grown out of the fact that

Pentecost has not been perpetuated," so a prominent minister is quoted as saying a generation ago.

Let it be said that the message of Pentecost is properly declared. When Pentecost is perpetuated, it means the presentation of all phases of Christianity and the Church. The highest type of Christian character will be developed. There will be a real missionary imperative. Stewardship will come in for a right emphasis. The Christian home will find its proper position. Every area of society will feel the impact of this gospel. There will be new preachers and new laymen in the wake of a new Pentecost.

This is something that cannot be self-contained. Its very nature demands the telling thereof. One immediate fruit of this experience at Pentecost was the witnessing to others around about. Those who are willing to propagate such a dynamic and glorious message may have been brought to the Kingdom for such a time as this. Then let them not fail Him, the Church, or this generation. While the message must relate to the needs of the present day, and while methods may need adaptation, yet it must be remembered that the message itself does not change and must be rooted and grounded in the Rock, which is eternal.

Truly, this truth is believed, possessed, and produced in the lives of multitudes in this day. Let there be reaffirmation of belief in the same. Let it be believed with all the heart. Then let it be told to men at home and abroad. Such new emphasis to this biblical and historic truth may well be the opening wedge to revival for which many are praying, pleading, and believing.

What Is the Evidence of the Holy Spirit?

by Alton J. Shea

The universal call from Christ, the Head of the Church, is for all of His followers to be joined in a worldwide witness to His lordship. St. Paul often expressed his deep sadness at the divisions among Christians and wrote several letters addressed to the problem. Are we in the evangelical and holiness fellowship failing to bring clear teaching from the Word on the New Testament doctrine of the Spirit?

The only hope for the individual believer, and for any Christian body, is to be constantly under correction by the Word of God. It is the Scriptures that renew the Church again and again, and feed and nourish believers to a wholesome, happy, healthy, and peaceful walk with God. The Christian life is not frenzy, agitation, seeking and never finding. It is righteousness, peace, and joy in the Holy Spirit (Romans 14:17).

A Promised Guide

The great promise of the Christian era is the provision that the Holy Spirit of God will cleanse, fill, anoint, and abide with every believer in a special way unknown in the Old Testament times. This is a distinctive and specific grace flowing from all that the Lord Jesus has done for us by coming in the flesh, dying, rising, and ascending to the Father. He sent to us, from Himself and from the Father, a universal Helper and Coach of the same kind as Himself.

In the same way that Jesus taught, explained, commanded, demonstrated, rebuked, led, pled, comforted, encouraged, and loved

His wondering followers, so He is still with us by the Holy Spirit, carrying on this same blessed ministry. We are convicted by the Spirit of our sins, born again of the Spirit in our conversion, constantly guided, coached, and helped by the Spirit into a fruitful discipleship. We are led from faith by the Spirit to full surrender (Romans 12:1-2), until there is no hindrance to a filling and anointing of the Spirit again and again (Acts 4:31).

The core of this teaching comes to us in the book of Galatians. A person comes to God by faith in Jesus for forgiveness of sins and adoption into the family of God. This true faith, which always involves obedience, is rewarded by the gift of the Spirit. The Christian life is faith all the way and a walk in the Spirit all the way.

Then the fruit of the Spirit begins to be seen in the life (Galatians 5:22). Paul declares the Christian way is not law keeping, but is being a new creature and demonstrating faith through love (Galatians 5:6; 6:15).

The heart of the Christian way is to have Christ *formed in you* (Galatians 4:19). The work of the Spirit is to see that the very essence of the Spirit of Jesus is created in the heart of the Christian. Then the fruit of this close union with Jesus, as the vine and the branches, will be noted by all. St. Paul was so convinced that the way of faith alone, and not law keeping, brought the miracle of the Spirit's work into the life of the Christian, that one day he had to face Peter sternly on the issue (Galatians 2:11).

The work of the Spirit, so central in the Christian era, could be lost completely for the believer if he trusted in his own good works. Ignorance here can lead to tragedy. It must not be.

Something Greater Than the Law

The book of Romans flowers out the seed-truth of Galatians. One can imagine the precocious scholar from Tarsus, would-be saint of the tribe of Benjamin, determined to be a "Pharisee of the Pharisees," diligent in his studies, a popular fellow and leader among the students, proudly strolling the streets of Jerusalem in his robes. He boasted of the great law of his nation, he gloried in it, he loved it, his conscience approved of it. But, horror of horrors! One day he found he could not keep it! He discovered another law of sin in his members overcoming every lofty resolve.

That moral dilemma haunted this young zealot, until one day he saw glory in the dying face of the martyr Stephen, and soon thereafter powerfully met the Lord of Glory himself. Here at last on the road to Damascus, he found the power to do what he could never do by himself. Here was the Spirit of life in Christ Jesus greater than the law of sin and death (Romans 8:2). Saul of Tarsus had come upon the greatest spiritual discovery of the ages—Christ in you, the hope of glory. Henceforth, he was a slave to Jesus.

Every Bible reader should prayerfully trace the key words of Romans 6—know, reckon, yield, obey. Then go on to meditate on the elements of the Spirit's ministries to the believer in Romans 8—victory over, and cleansing from, indwelling sin, certainty of sonship and inheritance, guidance, rescue from defeat and fear and weakness in prayer, infusion of hope for the future, and resolution of the overwhelming circumstances of life (Romans 8:28). That person will surely come to the flood tide of blessing that only a conqueror in Christ can know. Nothing, absolutely nothing, can separate such a soul from the love of God! And all this is the continuing work of the Spirit in the heart of the Christian right here on earth. How rich can the child of God be? Corrie ten Boom said that when the worst happens in the life of the child of God, the best remains.

Witness of the Spirit

What then is the sure evidence that the Holy Spirit is in the life of the believer? Is it the evidence of one or another of the gifts of the Spirit?

According to God's Word, the Spirit of life in Christ Jesus gives, above all, the power for cleansing and Christlikeness. It was Paul's prayer that God would *strengthen you with power through His Spirit in your inner being, so that Christ may dwell in your hearts through faith* (Ephesians 3:16-17).

Here is the healing, unity, and fellowship the modern Church needs today. We must rally around the indwelling Christ. To insist on any other criterion as indication of the Spirit's abiding is to go beyond the Word of God. People took knowledge of the early Spirit-filled disciples that they had been with Jesus, their Lord and Master, the Christ of the ages, and that they had learned of Him.

Humility
and Holiness

by Andrew Murray

"Keep away; don't come near me, for I am too sacred for you!" (Isaiah 65:5).

We speak of the holiness movement in our times, and praise God for it. We hear a great deal about seekers after holiness and professors of holiness, about holiness teaching and holiness meetings. The blessed truths of holiness in Christ and holiness by faith are being emphasized as never before. But the great test of whether or not the holiness we profess to seek or to attain is true, will be *whether it produces increasing humility.* In the creature, humility is the one thing needed to allow God's holiness to dwell in him and shine through him.

A Humble Heart

In Jesus, the Holy One of God Who makes us holy, a divine humility was the secret of His life and His death and His exaltation. The one infallible test of our holiness will be the humility before God and others which characterizes us. Humility is the bloom and the beauty of holiness.

The chief mark of counterfeit holiness is its lack of humility. Every seeker after holiness needs to be on guard lest, unconsciously, what was begun in the spirit will be perfected in the flesh, and pride will creep in where its presence is least expected.

Two men went up into the temple to pray. One was a Pharisee, the other a tax collector. There is no place or position so sacred but that the Pharisee can enter there. Pride can lift its head in the very temple of God and make His worship the scene of its self-exaltation. Since the time Christ exposed his pride, the Pharisee has put on the disguise of the tax collector, and both the confessor of deep sinfulness and the professor of the highest holiness must be on the watch. Just when we are most anxious to have our hearts be the temple of God, we shall find the two men coming up to pray. And the tax collector will find that his danger is not from the Pharisee beside him, who despises him, but the Pharisee within who commends and exalts him.

In God's temple, when we think we are in the holiest of all places, in the presence of His holiness, let us beware of pride. *One day the angels came to present themselves before the Lord, and Satan also came with them* (Job 1:6).

God, I thank You that I am not like other men—robbers, evildoers, adulterers—or even like this tax collector (Luke 18:11). It is in the things that give us a reason for thanksgiving, even in the very thanksgiving which we render to God, or in the confession that God has done it all, that self finds a reason for satisfaction. Yes, even in the temple, where only the language of penitence and trust in God's mercy are heard, the Pharisee may take up the note of praise, and, while thanking God, actually be congratulating himself. Pride can clothe itself in the garments of praise or of penitence. Even though the words *I am not like other men* are rejected and condemned, their spirit may too often be found in our feelings and language towards our fellow worshipers and others.

Would you like to know if this really is true? Just listen to the way in which churches and Christians often speak of one another— how little of the meekness and gentleness of Jesus there is. It is so little remembered that deep humility must be the keynote of what the servants of Jesus say about themselves or each other.

Are there not many churches or congregations, many missions or conventions, many societies or committees, even many missions among the heathen where the harmony has been disturbed and the work of God hindered, because those who are known as saints have proven by their touchiness and impatience, by their defensiveness and assertiveness, by their sharp judgments and unkind words, that they did not consider others to be better than themselves, and that their holiness has very little in it of the humility of the saints?

Keep away; don't come near me, for I am too sacred for you! (Isaiah 65:5). What a parody on holiness! Jesus, the Holy One, is the humble One. The holiest will always be the humblest. There is no one holy but God. We have as much of holiness as we have of God. And whatever we have of God will be the real measure of our humility, because humility is nothing but the disappearance of self in the vision that God is everything. The holiest will be the humblest.

Though the barefaced, boasting Israelite of the days of Isaiah is not often seen—our manners are better than to speak that way—that spirit is often still seen, both in our treatment of fellow Christians and of the children of the world. In the spirit in which opinions are given, and work is undertaken, and faults are exposed, very often, though the garb is that of the tax collector, the voice is still that of the Pharisee: *God, I thank You that I am not like other men.*

Is there such humility to be found that people still do consider themselves to be *less than the least of all saints,* the servants of all? There is. *Love does not boast, it is not proud. It is not rude, it is not self-seeking.*

A Servant's Spirit

When the spirit of love is poured out in the heart, when the divine nature comes to a full birth, when Christ, the meek and lowly Lamb of God, is truly formed within, then the power of a perfect love is given that forgets itself and finds its happiness in blessing others, in bearing with them and honoring them, however feeble they may be. Where this love enters, God enters. And when God has entered in His power, and revealed Himself as all, then the creature becomes nothing. And when the creature becomes nothing before God, it cannot be anything but humble towards others.

The presence of God becomes not a thing of times and seasons, but the covering under which the soul always dwells; and its deep humility before God becomes the holy place of His presence from which all its words and works proceed.

May God teach us that our thoughts and words and feelings toward others are His test of our humility towards Him, and that our humility before Him is the only power that can enable us to be always humble with others. Our humility must come from the life of Christ, the Lamb of God, within us.

Dangerous Pride

Let all teachers of holiness, whether in the pulpit or on the platform, and all seekers after holiness, whether in private or in public, take warning. There is no pride so dangerous—because none is so subtle and insidious—as the pride of holiness. It is not that a person always says, or even thinks, *Keep away, for I am too sacred for you!* No. In fact, the thought would be regarded as repulsive. But there grows up, subconsciously, a hidden habit of the soul, which feels satisfaction in its accomplishments and cannot help seeing how far advanced it is over others. It can be recognized, not always in any special self-promotion or self-congratulation, but simply in the absence of that deep self-abasement which is always the mark of the soul that has seen the glory of God (Job 42:5, 6; Isaiah 6:5). It reveals itself, not only in words or thoughts, but in a tone, a way of speaking of others, in which those who have the gift of spiritual discernment cannot help but recognize the power of self.

Even the world, with its keen eyes, notices it and points to it as proof that the claim of a heavenly life does not necessarily produce any heavenly fruit. O friends! Let us beware. Unless we, with each advance in what we consider to be holiness, give our attention to the increase of humility, we may find that we have been enjoying beautiful thoughts and feelings, solemn acts of consecration and faith, but that the only sure mark of the presence of God, the disappearance of self, was missing all the time.

Come and let us run to Jesus, and hide ourselves in Him until we are clothed with His humility. That alone is our holiness.

The Spiritual Edge
The Advantage of Entire Sanctification

by Jerry Brecheisen

W inners often refer to the *edge* or advantage they had over their competitors. Race car drivers refer to the *edge* that their particular brand of tires or fuel mixture gave them over other drivers. Sailors in international competition speak of the *edge* produced by the particular shape of their boat's hull or the trim of a sail. And Christians are not left without a spiritual *edge*, which enables them to live victoriously in this present age.

Christ revealed this to His disciples in a stately prayer only hours before the awful agony of Calvary. *For them I sanctify Myself, that they too may be truly sanctified* (John 17:19). To sanctify means to set apart for a holy use. Christ sanctified Himself for our redemption and sanctification.

The Edge Provided

The writer to Hebrew Christians gave this account:

> *The blood of goats and bulls and the ashes of a heifer sprinkled on those who are ceremonially unclean sanctify them so that they are outwardly clean. How much more, then, will the blood of Christ, Who through the eternal Spirit offered Himself unblemished to God, cleanse our consciences from acts that lead to death, so that we may serve the living God!* (Hebrews 9:13-14).

What a hundred Old Testament laws and bylaws could not accomplish, Christ did in a single act of submission to His Father's will. Human beings could not be good enough or holy enough to fill the requirements of an absolutely Holy God. In measureless love, that same Holiness stepped from the halls of heaven to the horrors of earth, to provide the spiritual *edge*.

In the person of His sinless Son, God solved the sanctification problem. *God made Him Who had no sin to be sin for us,* the writer advises (2 Corinthians 5:21). In one powerful act of consecration on Mount Calvary, Christ paid the penalty of our sinful past and provided the power for our spiritual future. Now, by the act of acknowledging our human need and accepting God's Divine provision, we can enjoy the experience that Christ agonized to supply.

The process begins when we are saved. We are "translated from the kingdom of darkness." We are spiritually adopted into God's family. *Initial sanctification* has begun. The process of becoming more like Christ and less like the world has been put into motion. That's *progressive sanctification.* Then comes the glorious moment when we are convinced of our needs, we confess every known sin to God, submit every known area of our lives to everything known of God, and ask for His cleansing and empowering. That is the moment of *entire sanctification.*

The same Apostle who saw *another law at work in the members of [his] body, waging war against the law of [his] mind and making [him] a prisoner of the law of sin* (Romans 7:23), later advised of the solution. *Offer your bodies as living sacrifices, holy and pleasing to God—this is your spiritual act of worship* (Romans 12:1). In a moment of faith we can die to a life of sinfulness and rise to a life of holiness. Neither of these acts is accomplished by self. What the law could not do, Christ did. What an *edge!*

The Edge in Action

But how does that play out on the dusty fields of this day when sin gets the headlines and saintliness gets a laugh? This day is different only in methods, but not in morality from the time of the disciples. That's why the *edge* Christ provided for His followers is so important. Notice the ingredients of our Lord's prayer for His own.

Unity

Jesus prayed *that all of them may be one* (John 17:21). The psalmist declared, *How good and pleasant it is when brothers live together in unity!* (Psalm 133:1). The story is told of one ol' boy who didn't feel well enough to attend his church's annual business meeting. He sent word, "Just tell 'em whatever they're for, I'm agin'!" How awful it is when brothers dwell in division.

In just a few hours in the loneliness of Calvary, Christ would make provision for the common bonding of His followers. A thousand local church disturbances to follow would march rebelliously over the walls of Christ's provision for a perfected love. On the cross, sanctified selflessness looked to an angry mob and said, *Father, forgive them.* Sanctified selflessness looked away from its wounds to the needs of a mother. *Dear woman, here is your son* (the Apostle John). And, *[John], here is your mother.*

Validity

Christ continued in prayer, *May they also be in Us so that the world may believe that You have sent Me* (John 17:21).

After the Old Testament Ark of the Covenant was stolen, the family of Eli, the priest, gave a symbolic name to their child. They called him Ichabod. *The glory has departed* (1 Samuel 4:21). Entire sanctification brings the glory of God to the believer's life. It says to a snickering world, "There is validity in the message of the Cross!" The Marines call for "A Few Good Men." In a time when several prominent prophets have fallen from their "high-chairs" in disgrace, the world is looking for "a few good men."

A life filled with the power and presence of a resurrected Christ has no room for the practices of a Savior-less society. *Live by the Spirit and you will not satisfy the desires of the sinful nature.* God provides an *edge* to the sanctified heart in the face of Satan's lures— in the home, the office, the school, and the factory.

Victory

Christ prayed again, *Father, I want those You have given Me to be with Me where I am, and to see My glory* (John 17:24).

The entirely sanctified heart has a clearer understanding of the gospel song, "This world is not my home, I'm just a-passin' through; my treasures are laid up somewhere beyond the blue." The disciples would rub shoulders with a crowd that groaned under a daily load of sin and a sense of awful finality. Christ prayed that, as they walked among that crowd, they would have an overwhelming sense of victory and eternity.

Entire sanctification offers an eternity *edge*. It knows the inner peace of dwelling in "heavenly places in Christ Jesus" even while living in a mortgaged, earthly home. It rejoices in the luxury of a God who "will supply all my needs according to His riches in glory by Christ Jesus," even when holding a pink slip from an earthly employer. It lifts its head above the shadows and clouds of time and sings, "Peace, peace, wonderful peace, coming down from the Father above; sweep over my spirit forever, I pray, in fathomless billows of love."

Christ didn't promise a constant giggle. There are some things that sadden the heart of the saint. Entire sanctification isn't isolation. It's insulation. He promised the *edge* of His presence and the continuing spiritual resources necessary for immediate—and final—victory.

Have you been entirely sanctified?

Too Few Spirit-Filled Christians!

by Clyde C. Dupin

R ecently I've been studying the book of Acts. I have been
tremendously impressed by the power of the Holy Spirit
demonstrated through the surrendered lives of the apostles. As I
observe their courage, power, joy, and holy living, the adequacy of the
Holy Spirit is confirmed. When I compare their evangelism with the
Church today, it hardly seems necessary to say that what the Church
needs most is the power of the Holy Spirit.

In the early days of D.L. Moody's evangelistic ministry, an
old man would often say to Mr. Moody, "Honor the Holy
Ghost." He never forgot that admonition and God blessed his
ministry. No person or church will succeed unless they honor the
Holy Spirit. Those who honor the Holy Spirit honestly and
scripturally cannot fail. Our ministry and witness will be barren
and merely routine unless they are made effective through the
power of the Spirit.

There is always the danger that holiness people will dwell only
on the crisis experience of being Spirit-filled. There must be this
moment of all-inclusive surrender when the Spirit fills and purifies
and empowers us for service. But this must be followed by a process
that involves carrying the validity of that surrender into every
succeeding moment of the eternal now, living, witnessing, and
loving in our generation.

John Wesley believed so strongly in the updated Spirit-filled life
that no testimony could be given in a class meeting when it was
more than a week old. When we witness about the fullness of the

Spirit or the sanctified life, the one important aspect is that the Holy Spirit now fully possesses us.

It is evident that these early Christians were dead to self and alive to Christ. The Apostle Paul uses strong language. His common terms are "crucify," "mortify," "put to death," "strip off," and others like them. I do not believe that a Christian can be much use to God until he is dead to self. He cannot live completely to the glory of God until the old selfish nature has been crucified.

The secret is expressed by Paul, *I have been crucified with Christ and I no longer live, but Christ lives in me* (Galatians 2:20). Jesus said, *If anyone would come after Me, he must deny himself and take up his cross daily and follow Me* (Luke 9:23).

We have a responsibility to evangelize our generation. This should be carried out in every phase of our church program and daily living. This task can never be done without Spirit-empowered Christians. Most of our attempts at evangelism, whether in revivals, church programs, or daily witnessing, fail. The reason is the obvious lack of the power of the Holy Spirit. The Bible says, *But you will receive power when the Holy Spirit comes on you* (Acts 1:8). The apostles had power to reveal Christ in their daily living. Even though they were not trained ministers, there was a boldness and power about their lives. The people were attracted to them and marveled at their devotion to Christ. *They took note that these men had been with Jesus* (Acts 4:13).

The most attractive thing to our lost, lonely, hurting world is to see people who bear the fruit of the Spirit. This is the only proof most people in our world will ever need to know that Christ is real.

Power for Evangelism

The Holy Spirit gives power for persuasive evangelism. I am convinced that unless the Holy Spirit fills, the human spirit will fail. There is much work being done today in His name, but there is often an absence of His power. It is possible to preach, sing, witness, and devote full time to church work and have it all come to nothing.

God wants to use our talents, abilities, and time, but they will only be worthwhile when they are totally surrendered and He gets all the glory. In the second chapter of Acts, the Christians had such persuasive power that people were convicted and said, *Brothers, what shall we do?* (Acts 2:37).

Power for Growth

The Holy Spirit gives the power needed for church growth. These Spirit-filled disciples were concerned about reaching the lost. They shared their faith daily. They lived in a spirit of unity. This is necessary for any church to have, in order to attract the lost. Their joy was evident and made them attractive to the unsaved. As a result of this Spirit-filled ministry, *the Lord added to their number daily those who were being saved* (Acts 2:47).

Power to Persevere

The power of the Holy Spirit was the compelling force for continued evangelism. It was this power that kept them from defeat and self-pity when they were rebuffed and even beaten. They could even rejoice that they were counted worthy to suffer shame for His name. Only the Holy Spirit can give this kind of joy and victory. This sounds so different from the excuses I hear so often among church people.

The task of reaching our generation can never be accomplished apart from the supernatural power of the Holy Spirit. It is only the Holy Spirit who will keep us motivated and concerned for the lost. The secret of the early church is expressed in Acts 5:42: *Day after day, in the temple courts and from house to house, they never stopped teaching and proclaiming the good news that Jesus is the Christ.*

Without doubt, we have the message that our generation needs. But do we have the power to deliver that message? The power is not wrapped up in a correct theological statement, but in the person of the Holy Spirit. This message of full salvation can only be transmitted effectively through people who are filled with the Holy Spirit. All the essentials we need to reach our lost world are available with one exception: There are too few Spirit-filled Christians!

He Preached Holiness

by Dow Chamberlain

A reflection upon the life of Rev. Ray W. Chamberlain, as given by his youngest son at his funeral service on January 5, 1998:

Brothers and sisters, most of Daddy's friends and family could not be here today . . . because Daddy joined them in the Church above last Friday.

Daddy was remarkably blessed to be the son of a man who was a great singer, and a mother who was a skilled musician. To those natural gifts, he added skill in performance at juggling, walking on his hands, and an overall capacity to be a ham. As the leader of a jazz band, he seemed destined to be an entertainer. But God steered him in a different direction.

After three years of college and after working at Pontiac Motors, making wooden wheels, he learned to work with wood in his brother-in-law's sawmill. He got involved in printing and became highly skilled as a monotypist. It seemed that he would spend his life in printing. But, under the ministry of Joseph H. Smith, God turned his life away from a religion of conformity and nominal Christianity, and one Easter Sunday morning, he received the assurance of his salvation through faith alone.

What can I say about my father that he would find acceptable? I could recall his remarkable career as a printer, educator, singer, musician, builder, missionary, evangelist, author, editor, administrator, world traveler, pastor, churchman, father of six, grandfather of 26 and great-grandfather of 50. But I know what he would want me to talk about—that he entered the ministry as a *second* career and served the Lord for over sixty years after his ordination.

Called to Holiness

To be faithful to my father, I will have to speak of holiness. After his spiritual awakening, he journeyed from Davenport, Iowa, to Eaton Rapids, Michigan. At a camp meeting, he became involved in the holiness movement within Methodism. He began to understand that salvation meant more than forgiveness of sin, that salvation was a call to holiness, to godliness, and to the desire to be perfect in love in this life. And it is this belief which informed the rest of his life.

As a little boy, I heard him sing, "I'd rather have Jesus." I came to understand that this was not just a song that displayed his considerable vocal talents, but that his life was one of total devotion to holiness. This song really expressed his way of life. Holiness of life was not a burden or sacrifice. It was an unending love affair with his Lord. And when he sang, "When I look on His face, I'll wish I had given Him more," this was not mere spiritual hyperbole. Knowing how God had saved him from a life of futility, there was no way he could ever love God enough.

As a child, I was amazed at his capacity for discipline and work. He had a huge library—5,000 volumes at its peak. It seemed that from five in the morning to eleven at night, he was always occupied. It was not until I stood before my bishop to answer the historic questions asked of all preachers seeking full connection that it dawned on me that my father had been living according to that discipline as long as I had known him.

> *Have you faith in Christ?*
> *Are you going on to perfection?*
> *Are you earnestly seeking after it?*
> *Do you expect to be made perfect in love in this life?*
> *Will you visit from house to house?*
> *Will you teach the children in every place?*
> *Will you employ all your time in the ministry of God?*
> *Will you never be triflingly employed?*
> *Will you spend no more time in any one place than necessary?*
> *Will you always do everything exactly at the time?*
> *Will you not be in debt so as to embarrass your ministry?*

And the questions that were paraphrased in our family, "Will you do right because it is right and not because you have to?" *Will you keep these rules not for fear but for conscience's sake?*

I then began to understand why he read the entire works of Adam Clarke from cover to cover and why he always had a book tucked in his pocket. It was so that if he had as much as five minutes, he could be reading. This was not because he was a "type A" personality. The fact that he lived to 95 is evidence he was not a driven man. Instead, he was a man who was drawn, drawn by the love of God for him. That aroused love in his heart for God, and with that love for God, an intense desire to be as whole, as complete, as mature, as competent, as caring, as productive as God called him to be. Holiness was not an abstract idea. Holiness was God's Spirit incarnate in his vessel of clay.

Holiness Put Into Practice

Holiness did not make him a cautious, repressed soul paralyzed by the fear of what others might think. When a missionary colleague told Dad that he didn't want to ride into Kingston, the man used a racial slur, saying that he didn't want to ride with "them." Daddy said, "Then I guess you'll have to take the bus." Even though he was a Southerner—when he got religion, it brought an end to racial bigotry and pride. He could never understand why persons would insist on an instantaneous work of grace and then insist on gradualism when it came to racial equality. He was absolutely fearless and impartial. He saw no reason to give special treatment to persons who thought they were important.

Holiness meant that he would go anywhere and do anything. There was no task too humble nor any challenge too great. As Wesley wrote, "Sometimes we may please God and please ourselves, other times we can please God only by denying ourselves." He always received with thanksgiving what was provided him. That was everything from grits and gravy to mare's milk in Egypt, a tumbler full of fish eyes in the Philippines, sushi in Japan, and bull's blood clotted with urine. If people set it before him, he ate it with thanksgiving—as St. Paul said, *Eat what is set before you without question for conscience's sake.* He didn't ask questions for other reasons, as well.

The Freedom of Holiness

Holiness meant that he was always amazed at the beautiful. No matter where he went, he enjoyed everything around him. He enjoyed people; he was open to their differences. His only complaint was that he found it impossible to love Arabic music, which he insisted was sung in the key of "Z flat."

Holiness enabled him to be serious about his task, but never take himself too seriously. We all know his laugh: sort of a cross between a crowing rooster and a laughing hyena. Although he didn't play games often, he was always playful, with a childlike curiosity for new gadgets and gimmicks.

The most remarkable thing to me was that when he turned 58, an age when other preachers I knew were planning on retirement to fish and play golf, Daddy began a whole new career—world missionary evangelism. As he explained it, earlier in life he had many things he *loved* to do and many things he *had* to do. Now he was free to do what he really felt that he loved to do.

And everywhere he went he preached holiness. Holiness, to him, was not a piece of chrome, which can be added to dress up the basic model of Christianity. What he discovered is that Buddhists, Muslims, Hindus, animists, and semi-pagans all had a theology related to the forgiveness of sin. What was lacking was a doctrine of the immanent presence of God in human life, which brought harmony, peace, and reunion with God. His primary message was not how to have sins forgiven. People didn't need Christianity for that. He could not even tell people that the Bible said this or that, because the Bible was not their holy book. But he gave witness to the peace and joy God had brought to his heart. He preached that the inner life could be made pure and holy and that all of life could be filled with divine presence. This message makes broken heartstrings vibrate once more.

Holiness filled his life with confidence. One of the spirituals he wrote says,

> "I never put a thing in the good Lord's hands,
> But what it turned out just right."

When I think of the difficult situations that were given to him in serving the Lord, and when I think of his sufferings and labors, I know he didn't run on mere compassion or pity. His life was not lived for duty and honor alone. He was simply doing what he believed God called him to do. And he knew that, as long as he was doing what God asked him to do, it was God's job to take care of him. And because taking care of him was God's job, he never spent his time taking care of himself. He never asked anything for himself. He didn't have to own a fancy car. Even when in London, he never visited Saville Row. He never had a fancy study or luxurious house. He just served the Lord he loved.

John Wesley said that Methodists die well. People who live well can die well, too. As Daddy lay on his deathbed and we gathered around to anoint him and share in the holy Eucharist, I knew he had prayed mightily that God would heal him. God had healed him so many times before. But he put it in God's hands. And I believe it turned out just right.

Has he increased in holiness as well as in wealth? If not, he has made a poor exchange.

—John Wesley

Authentic Holiness
at Home

by Denis Applebee

Some people are so holy that you can't live with them! What I mean is that some people see themselves as keeping such a high standard of righteousness, punctuality and perfection that no one can be at ease in their presence. There is no doubt that no one can stand in the light of God's holiness without shaded eye and bent knee. Yet when that same God stepped down to this earth, He laid aside His glory, but not His holiness. The holiness of Jesus, the Man, was such that sinners felt at ease and only hypocrites felt compelled to leave the room.

Never before have homes been so adorned, comfortable, and relaxing in their furnishings. Yet they could easily be furniture stores with their owners simply passing through. Young people often choose to live in a run-down apartment with their friends, rather than come home to a Christian parental glass case. They don't fit, and they feel it!

I have seen a generation lost to holiness homes because the translation of the doctrine of perfect love left off the word love. Out of the fear of compromise or criticism, a standard was maintained which made children grow up to hate the very word *holiness.*

How different it is where God the Holy Spirit has been more than a doctrine or a one-time experience. In these homes, holiness has been a warm, attractive, understanding, growing life, which takes into its orbit the changes, styles, and music of teenage years as it patiently bears the fruit of the Spirit. Such a lifestyle tempts hungry hearts to seek and find what it has enjoyed. Is it possible? Yes, of course it is!

Open-Mindedness

First, there must be an honest assessment of the times before God, rather than before other Christians. Many of the changes that have come with each generation have been condemned by the Church, only to be accepted later. If we will be honest and sit down with a young person and find out what the real issue is, we will be better able to teach them and maybe learn a little ourselves.

Holiness in the home must have healthy thinking in order to arrive at convictions that are based on Scripture and not tradition— convictions that are firsthand. This builds trust into our family relationships because the young member of the family then knows that words are spoken out of thoughtful obedience to God, and not mindless prejudice.

Honest Relationships

Jesus had terrible things to say to those whom He called "whitewashed tombs." Inner holiness produces the most attractive lives where it really counts—in the home. It results from of a vital relationship with God in which the heart, with all its motives, is cleansed. This, in turn, produces right relationships with our spouses and children.

Impatience is dealt with. Selfishness is dealt with. This is not done by some surgical removal of these individual sins, but through an experience in which we face what we really are on the inside, and let God deal with what hinders the fruit of the Spirit.

Such an experience may come, and has to some, long after we experienced a more basic experience of sanctifying grace. Although that mighty work freed our hearts to obey God and established us in our walk with Him, we had to face each new situation and respond to it with honesty. If we have sinned before our spouses or children, then we need to make a confession. This will not cause them to doubt our experience, but believe in it. For they will see God at work in our lives in true holiness which humbles and restores. Home will be a place of understanding, compassion, authenticity, and— dare we say it—heaven on earth in which to live.

Expression

Has the holiness movement suffered over past decades because of a failure to communicate? John and Charles Wesley were masters at the art of communication. The fire of their experience was turned loose in word and verse. Other early preachers of holiness were giants in the pulpit, drawing men and women to the altar of consecration.

But where are the communicators of holiness in our day? Who will stand and bear witness to the transforming nature of full salvation? Let holiness be lived, yes. And let it also be preached. Let us give clear and bold expression to the marvelous, scriptural truth: *It is God's will that you should be sanctified.*

O for a Heart to Praise My God

O for a heart to praise my God,
a heart from sin set free,
a heart that always feels Thy blood
so freely shed for me.

A heart resigned, submissive, meek,
my great Redeemer's throne,
where only Christ is heard to speak,
where Jesus reigns alone.

A humble, lowly, contrite heart,
believing, true, and clean,
which neither life nor death can part
from Him that dwells within.

—Charles Wesley

Hope for the Holiness Message

by Keith Drury

Though we need to honestly admit that the holiness *movement* is dead, the holiness *message* is quite alive. In fact, I believe it is about to make a comeback. There are at least four encouraging signs that we may see a revival of the holiness message in our lifetime.

The Current Ferment in Holiness Churches

Holiness churches are stewing about holiness. We are talking about holiness again, even arguing about it. Dutiful recitation of the old holiness shibboleths is being replaced by honest self-examination. We have admitted that we are no longer a holiness movement, but we've lost something in that process. Middle-aged Baby Boomers now wonder if they threw out too much treasure with the trash. Our colleges are holding conferences on holiness. District ministerials are focusing on holiness and holy living. All change is rooted in confession. All this ferment should encourage us! If we get enough ferment, maybe we'll get some new wine!

135

Biblical Truth Always Resurfaces

The holiness message is not dead. It is suppressed. And it is about to resurface. Why? Because holiness is a *biblical* truth. Holiness is not a denominational distinctive or pet doctrine. Holiness is biblical. Suppressing a biblical truth is like hiding a cork under water. Sooner or later it always pops to the surface.

Perhaps we are at the tail end of a cycle of doctrinal excesses. Doctrines have a way of almost disappearing before being rediscovered. The pattern seems so obvious when we look backwards. First, a timeless truth is "discovered" and *propagated.* The truth soon spreads wildly as the solution to a present dilemma (in the case of holiness, sin-bent, half-saved Christians). The doctrine and experience moves rapidly across denominational lines as the effective solution to the problem of carnal, immature, powerless Christians. But, sooner or later, excesses are introduced—"If a little is good, more is better." In our case, the excesses of emotionalism, non-biblical folk theology, and coldhearted legalism eventually emerged. Finally, when the excesses are full-grown, they ignite a reaction, especially in the next generation. In the reaction stage, the new generation assents to the written doctrine, but internally rejects its premise. All they can see are the excesses. Their preaching and teaching on holiness is primarily about correcting the past excesses, not propagating the basic truth. Ironically, the corrective eventually becomes the doctrine! The doctrine itself is now shoved underwater. It is hidden, and we go on to other things.

But repressing a biblical doctrine will not last. Ignoring the doctrine of holiness has, over time, produced an inadequate God concept, confusion about the judgment side of the gospel, an insufficient doctrine of conversion, and a strain of Christians who are worldly, half-committed, half-hearted . . . half-saved. Holiness will always come back—because it is in the Bible.

The Massive Shift Under Way in American Culture

We are right smack in the middle of a massive cultural shift in America. Yesterday's conservatives have become today's moderates. Television has discovered pastors' and preachers' wives! Bill Bennett's *The Book of Virtues* became a best-seller in secular America.

Victimization is out of style and responsibility is in. *Newsweek* even ran a cover story recommending the return of shame and guilt, and suggesting that we should again adopt the term *sin!*

The culture is shifting. Could it be that the Lord is moving the entire culture of America? Could God be providing the right conditions for His people to return to His basic truths of repentance, godliness, righteousness, and holiness? Whatever He is up to, we who value the holiness message should be delighted at the massive cultural shifts under way right now, for they provide an ideal atmosphere for the growth and expansion of the holiness message. That should encourage us!

The Back-to-Basics Move Among Evangelicals

While there is a shift in the general culture in America, there is also a major shift under way in the evangelical subculture. A back-to-basics movement is quickly gaining momentum. Evangelicals are turning back to the Bible, doctrine, theology, and even church history. "How to" books are declining. Classics are gaining. The moral collapse of many evangelical leaders has had a sobering effect. Watch the terms in the evangelical world today, and you will see words like integrity, virtue, principles, accountability, and character. There is growing concern for the great host of church members who are not saved. Pastors are concerned at the alarming number of people totally unchanged by their "conversion." There is a growing "remnant movement." There is hunger across the church for authenticity and godliness. Books on holiness now sell strongly outside the holiness movement. Major evangelical publishers seek books on the deeper life, spiritual disciplines, and godliness. And by no means least, a Christian men's movement sprang up based on propositions of obedience, accountability, sexual purity, obeying the Great Commission and following the Great Commandment, all essentially holiness emphases. Is this not the work of God in creating a new holiness movement?

Is God leading shifts in both the world and Church to provide the restoration of this biblical truth? Are we not more like England in Wesley's time than ever in our history? We holiness people are ready for such a renewal, aren't we?

Let it rain, Lord! Let it rain!

Incandescent Christians

by George E. Failing

Many Christians reflect some of the light of the gospel, but few manifest its *heat.* Yet the Word urges us to keep our *spiritual fervor* (fire, in Greek) as we serve the Lord (Romans 12:11). Light can attract attention and reveal objects, but fire can protect us and destroy enemies. When Ananias and Sapphira brought their partial gifts, representing them as the whole, they fell down dead and great fear came upon the church (who wants to join that church unless they are totally committed?) as well as upon outsiders. But Scripture immediately states that the purging of pretending Christians from the church resulted in increase: *more and more men and women believed in the Lord* (Acts 5:14).

Holy Fire

Christian testimony cannot be fully proclaimed and protected without the "heat" of the Holy Spirit. Jesus Himself affirmed that those in the Upper Room were to be baptized with the Holy Ghost. His evidences on Pentecost Day were wind and fire—wind to distribute the blessing and fire to consume the inward dross.

As light only, the Christian doctrines may be compared with other religions. But as fire, the Christian faith stands alone. *The god who answers by fire—He is God* (1 Kings 18:24).

Of John the Baptist, believers said, *John was a lamp that burned and gave light* (John 5:35). That is, the truth John preached was on fire, though John did no miracles. Incandescent means light by means of heat. To the Laodicean church, Jesus said, "I want you to be cold or hot." Lukewarmness, or cool light, does not issue from the God who is a *consuming fire.*

The earliest sacrifice was offered to God by Abel, by fire. Abraham's consecration to God was sealed when *a smoking firepot with a blazing torch appeared and passed between the pieces* (Genesis 15:17). All Old Testament offerings that dealt with sin and/or consecration (both sin and burnt offerings) were to be consumed by fire. The light of God's presence in the Tabernacle was not to be extinguished: *The fire must be kept burning on the altar continuously; it must not go out* (Leviticus 6:13).

Some Christians have never been taught that they may be incandescent—burn as well as shine. After Pentecost, Paul found at Ephesus disciples of the Lord who had known only of the baptism of John, not the fiery baptism of the Spirit. They were doubtless saved, but were not burning witnesses. Only those who are willing to hazard worldly goods and life itself can be called incandescent Christians (Acts 15:26). Men do not fear light alone as much as heat. A Christian testimony that does not bring fear upon the ungodly does not restrain evil.

Moses did not become the deliverer of Israel until he saw the bush that burned! Out of that burning bush God spoke. It is evident that no preacher can proclaim God's truth as he ought until he has felt God's fire. It was the fire of the Spirit as light that illuminated Peter's mind at Pentecost, while it was the fire of the Spirit as heat that carried conviction to the hearts of those Jews gathered at Jerusalem—*Brothers, what shall we do?*

Paul urges Timothy to *fan into flame the gift of God* (2 Timothy 1:6). And all Christians are commanded, *Do not put out the Spirit's fire* (1 Thessalonians 5:19). To self-satisfied Christians, Jesus said, *so be earnest* (fiery, in Greek), *and repent* (Revelation 3:19). Too many Christians have joined forces with moral activists who want to reform our vile society and believe that they are accomplishing a great mission for God. If Christians are joined in these efforts by "good citizens" who themselves are unregenerate, they feel compensated when some laws are changed and some sinful practices are condemned. But no regenerative results flow from these efforts. The "good man," unsaved, goes to the same hell as the harlot and the murderer. Only by full trust in Christ as the only Savior can any person be saved. Better societies do not go to heaven. Only radically converted sinners do.

Light Without Heat

I may be judging too harshly, but it seems to me that too many of us, ministers and laymen, have come to be content with the light that has no heat. We are fluorescent, not incandescent Christians. If what Jesus said to the Laodiceans applies to us, we are only lukewarm. And lukewarm Christians He will *spit out.* Are we no longer willing to be incandescent for Christ? Are we satisfied with conventions, larger congregations, greater giving, counseling, festivals, and celebrations of various sorts? These are indeed associated with religious activities, but are they related to Calvary and to Pentecost? Do they not pander to the "updated" world we live in, rather than cause us to devote ourselves to God's kingdom, now and forever?

Perhaps Isaiah's questions and answers should concern us: Who among us shall dwell with the devouring fire? Who among us shall dwell with everlasting burnings? ("The fire of heaven is love; the fire of hell is wrath"—GEF.) *He who walks righteously and speaks what is right, who rejects gain from extortion . . . this is the man who will dwell on the heights, whose refuge will be the mountain fortress . . . Your eyes will see the King in His beauty and view a land that stretches afar* (Isaiah 33:15-17).

That's the land of the unclouded day!

As for me, I want to be an incandescent Christian—and teacher of the Word.

Preaching Holiness

by David E. Wilson

There can be no doubt from the plain teaching of the Word of God, that we must be made holy in order to please and glorify God. In the Old Testament, the command is given to be holy. Leviticus 11:44, *Be holy, because I am holy.* Exodus 22:31, *You are to be my holy people.* In the New Testament, we are similarly called to holiness. First Thessalonians 4:7, *For God did not call us to be impure, but to live a holy life.* And 1 Peter 1:15, *But as He who called you is holy, so be holy in all you do.* In the gospel, which is *the power of God for salvation for everyone that believes,* we have both the obligation and the authority to proclaim to everyone this glorious message that has power to help us retrieve by grace through faith the likeness in holiness.

The Possibility of Holiness

If God has called us to holiness then certainly His call makes possible the attainment. God's commands are His enablements, thereby giving assurance that whatever is required can be fulfilled. First Thessalonians 5:23-24 is an example of the authority we are given to preach this great message and the manner by which we are made holy: *May God Himself, the God of peace, sanctify you through and through. May your whole spirit, soul and body be kept blameless at the coming of our Lord Jesus Christ. The one who calls you is faithful and He will do it.*

The Holiness of God

In view of the many theories concerning holiness that are being preached, great care should be taken as to whose holiness should be sought. Obviously, it is not the "holiness" of some denomination, group, institution, or man. It is beautifully stated in Hebrews 12:10 as *His holiness*. The context of the verse promises that those who will submit to the discipline of the Lord shall partake of His holiness and be enabled to measure up to the commands of the Lord to "be holy." Unfortunately, in some of the messages being preached on the subject, one would get the impression that there were several kinds of holiness. There is but one, the *holiness of God.*

Peculiar tags with personal ideas attached, opinions with claims not promised in the Scriptures, and strained interpretations are not conducive to one's seeking for this experience. Great care should be taken in the preaching of this wonderful message, which has rightly been called "the central idea of Christianity." The main theme should be sound doctrine, emphasizing the reality and power of the blood of Christ, to make possible a blessed recovery to the spiritual likeness of God, here and now.

Trying to make the necessary conditions to receiving the experience too easy by taking a position of compromise, will tend to a lowering of the beauty of holiness in life and action.

Some extreme positions have been preached. Among those are Adamic Perfection—the state that Adam enjoyed before the fall; Angelic Perfection—the perfection of angels in an unfallen state; and Absolute Perfection—which belongs only to God. May we ever make it clear that this glorious doctrine with its message of hope partakes of none of those extremes.

The Reality of Holiness

There is a blessed Christian Perfection—a grand experience obtainable here and now for the honest soul, that makes it possible for us to meet the scriptural demand, *Be holy.*

Aside from the command of Scriptures the result, produced wherever the message is clearly presented, is a reason for preaching this wonderful truth. All classes are challenged and affected. Does it not cause the sinner to sense the holiness of God in a new light, with a realization of the great difference between him and his Savior?

To the saved, it is at once a challenge and a privilege. The born again, walking in light thrown on their pathways, yearn for the "fullness of the Spirit" with an accompanying longing for soul rest and calm in the midst of the storms of life.

To the Church naturally comes the challenge of being like Him with an appreciation of the possibilities in the undeveloped soul realm. The incoming of the Holy Spirit as an Abiding Guest will result in a sense of new strength and the development of latent power.

Inasmuch as we are living in the Holy Spirit's dispensation and He is the active Agent of the godhead on earth, obviously the message of a Spirit-filled life is in order. Wherever this message is faithfully preached, the Church becomes aggressive, souls are blessed, and revival will begin.

The Word locates sin in the soul, not in the corporeal body. The words "flesh" and "body" are used in Scriptures to mean man's unsanctified, carnal spiritual nature. The hand or foot of a man can no more sin than the house he lives in or the dagger he strikes with. It is as ridiculous to talk of sin being in the material flesh as it would be to locate it in one's boots or coat or carriage.

—Martin W. Knapp

The Gift
of Pentecost—
The Holy Spirit

by Virgil A. Mitchell

Pentecost Sunday commemorates one of the most significant events in Christian history. There never has been such a day as Pentecost—either before or since. The Christian Church was launched when the promised Holy Ghost was poured out upon the 120 in the upper room in Jerusalem. The dispensation of the Holy Spirit began. The executive of the Trinity came to make effective all that Calvary had provided. The Holy Spirit is the ultimate fact of revelation and the unique force in redemption.

The Holy Spirit had His place in Old Testament times. He brooded over the void of the earth, bringing order out of chaos. However, on the day of Pentecost, He began, among other things, to convict sinners, regenerate penitents, sanctify believers, empower Christians, and lead His followers. He glorifies Christ by making Him real to His children. Daniel Steele observes:

> The Spirit in the believer testifies of Jesus, that He has ascended on high and that He is the Mediator between God and man. . . . After the ascension, wherever there was a believer there was an omnipotent Christ. A thousand cities might simultaneously behold the display of His power. On the day of Pentecost, a thousand of the fiercest enemies of Christ laid down their weapons and proclaimed Him Lord to the glory of God the Father. The hearts of His own immediate disciples . . . having been brought into complete subjection by the outpouring of the Holy Spirit from the

throne of their risen Lord, went forth conquering and to conquer.

The Power of Pentecost

The historic Pentecost never will be repeated. It need not be, any more than Calvary should be repeated. The provisions of Pentecost, however, can and should be appropriated daily. Christ said, *But you will receive power when the Holy Spirit comes on you; and you will be My witnesses in Jerusalem, and in all Judea and Samaria, and to the ends of the earth* (Acts 1:8).

His disciples already possessed miracle-working power. They had cast out devils, healed the sick, and cleansed the lepers. Thus it was not this kind of power of which He was speaking. It was power to live a holy life in an unholy world. They were to be adequately equipped to face the onslaughts of Satan in his plan to stamp out the young church.

The fiery persecution unleashed against the church took its toll in physical life and, in some instances, the followers of Christ succumbed to the cruel and intimidating efforts of Satan. Those who daily and hourly appropriated the power of the Holy Spirit triumphed over the worst the Devil could hurl at them. A new dimension of living had been introduced. This enduement of power caused their foes to recognize they had been with Jesus.

Through the power of the Holy Spirit, the Church overran her foes, battered down her opposition, and established herself upon an unshakable foundation. This gift of power to live a holy life is available to the Church today. It must be appropriated by faith and demonstrated in daily living.

Christ not only commanded us to be holy; He provided the Agent to make us holy—the outpoured Holy Spirit. Peter explained what happened on the day of Pentecost: *God, who knows the heart, showed that He accepted them by giving the Holy Spirit to them, just as He did to us. He made no distinction between us and them, for He purified their hearts by faith* (Acts 15:8, 9).

Holy Spirit Baptism

Purity of heart, sanctification, crucifixion of the old man of sin, and cleansing from the carnal mind result from the baptism of the

Holy Spirit. The holiness of God is imparted to the heart of the seeker through the ministry of the Holy Spirit, and by daily appropriating the grace of God, he is thereby enabled to live a holy life. The experience of holiness is thus a crisis and a continuing process.

The baptism of the Holy Spirit is as essential today as on the day of Pentecost. The Church has succeeded or failed in the direct proportion that this baptism has been received or rejected. The great need of the Church today is to recapture the message, receive the experience, and live a life of the Holy Spirit's fullness. This is a divine work of grace, instantaneously received subsequent to regeneration. It cleanses the heart from sin. The evidence of being filled with the Spirit is an inward witness whereby God's Spirit witnesses or testifies to man's spirit, and man's spirit accepts God's witness that the Holy Spirit has taken up His abode in the heart. This issues in a holy life, producing the fruit of the Spirit, which is *love, joy, peace, patience, kindness, goodness, faithfulness, gentleness and self-control* (Galatians 5:22, 23)

Christ was also speaking of power to witness. He said, *But you will receive power when the Holy Spirit comes on you; and you will be My witnesses* (Acts 1:8). Note that it is not *shall become* or *should become*, but *will be*. The root of the word *witness* is *martyr*. The responsibility of a witness is to tell what he knows, tell it in as effective a manner as possible, and to live such a life that when the witness is given, people will believe what he says. The Holy Spirit is essential to accomplish this.

The experience Pentecost provides must not only be received and enjoyed; it must be declared. It must be proclaimed, explained, and shared with others. Equipment for this ministry is the daily appropriation of the power of the Holy Spirit. Observe the elements that made effective the witness of the early Church as revealed in the book of Acts: unbroken fellowship (2:42), fullness of joy and gladness (2:46-47), intercessory prayer (2:42, 46; 6:1-4), generosity in support of the gospel (2:44-45), complete dedication to God and His cause (5:41-42), the continual filling of the Holy Spirit (4:8, 31; 6:3, 5; 7:55; 9:17; 13:9, 52), and constantly witnessing to their faith in Christ (3:1-26; 4:1-3; 5:19-28; 5:32). In fact, this method involved the total Church in its total task.

By life, by lip, and by pen this witness must be given today if we are to perpetuate, propagate, and give dynamic proof that the Holy Spirit is at work in the Church. Have you received your personal Pentecost?

Spiritual Channels That Run Deep

by Harry Wood

"American Christianity is like a river—a river that is a mile wide and an inch deep."

That classic diagnosis by a European theologian has been quoted often. Remember, however, that observation was given decades ago, long before the current spiritual drought. The only alteration might be that the width and depth are overstated for these times.

Examining the spiritual status of an existing culture can be tricky. A word of caution may be appropriate. Elijah discovered long ago that it isn't always easy to make an accurate spiritual assessment of one's own generation. The tendency exists to inflate our self-evaluation while downgrading that of those about us. We are always dependent on God's perspective when attempting a spiritual appraisal.

Some Are Faithful

But even in the worst of times, there remain spiritual channels that run deep: people who are true saints of God. They may be unknown to us, hidden behind obscurity or humility, but they remain prominent in the eyes of the Omniscient One.

That the appraisal process is challenging, however, does not remove the necessity from us. We cannot close our eyes and ears to what is occurring about us. While spiritual shallowness and lack of commitment are common terms used to diagnose our present spiritual condition, I am convinced that they describe symptoms rather than causes. Paul's words to the Philippians come to mind, *Therefore, my dear friends, as you have always obeyed—not only in my presence, but now much more in my absence—continue to work out your salvation with fear and trembling, for it is God Who works in you to will and to act according to His good purpose.*

The Greek word for will in this passage is *thelo*. In its common usage there are four basic meanings: to have an inclination or compulsion, to be motivated with desire, or to have intent, or a resolve based on a decision. Obviously, before we act, *to act according to His good purpose, thelo* must be present within us.

Have we somehow lost our "will to do"? If so, why? Has God withdrawn the motivation from us? Have we suppressed it until we have struck a deathblow to it? Or has the Church perhaps suffocated it?

Before drawing any premature conclusions, visit another passage with me to expand our sensitivities. Paul wrote to the Galatians, *So I say, live by the Spirit, and you will not gratify the desires of the sinful nature. For the sinful nature desires what is contrary to the Spirit, and the Spirit what is contrary to the sinful nature. They are in conflict with each other, so that you do not do what you want.*

A collision of influences occurs within our wills. The desire of God stimulated in us runs headlong into *the desires of the sinful nature* that war against the Spirit of God. There is a spiritual tug-of-war going within the human heart—two sources of influence seeking to fashion the prevailing motivation.

Spiritual Depth

Obviously, the Spirit of God does not forcibly dictate the conclusion of the battle within. Otherwise, all people would be ruled by godly passions. Thus, it would be presumptuous for us to assume that we can decree the outcome. You cannot force someone to will or to be spiritually deep any more than you can force someone to be healthy. It is feasible, however, to provide an atmosphere and diet that greatly enhance that possibility. This is achieved through spiritual dynamics, and not legalistic pressures. There are five key elements that I believe can contribute to arousing and enhancing motivation for spiritual depth. They are exposure, experience, expectation, exercise, and earnestness.

My father became severely ill as a young man. He went to the doctor and was treated for an acute case of arthritis. The treatment seemed thorough and thoughtful. He was given books to read about arthritis and its consequences. A special diet was accepted and adhered to for quite some time. There was extensive therapy, and many treatments were given for his agonizing condition. He made regular doctor visits, and gradually he was even issued a cane to support his ailing body. But he eventually died . . . of bone cancer.

Sincerity, compassion, and effort are never an adequate substitute for truth. Truth, no matter how much it hurts or offends, is necessary for an accurate diagnosis. An accurate diagnosis is vital for effective treatment.

The Sin Problem

Somehow, we must come to grips with the fact that the underlying concern in all of this is our sin problem. Sin is a word that stirs many allergic reactions. Sometimes we would rather give a false diagnosis than be associated with the word sin. But spiritual and biblical integrity demand the honest exposure of our sin problem.

John Fischer is right:

> Sin is not only the act I did, it's the motivation that made me do what I did. Sin is both the nature and the deed. To a point, I can do something about the deed. I can compare my deeds to everyone else's deeds and arrange them to produce satisfactory results. I can fiddle with the law a bit to adjust it to the deed, but something keeps cropping up. Something deep inside me is the source of the deed, like bad water that resists all attempts at purification . . . it's not bad influence—it's a bad beginning. There's something fundamentally wrong inside—something fighting against the right thing to do. And though we know this is true, we prefer to surround ourselves with those who would give us a better report.

We have a sin problem that will not be resolved through a merely therapeutic ministry, educational process, positive mental attitude, or gifts discovery. Regardless of our styles of worship or philosophies of ministry, sin must be dealt with at the foot of the Cross through the blood of Jesus Christ. Sin must be exposed, then we can *confess our sins* and discover that *He is faithful and just and will forgive us our sins and cleanse us from all unrighteousness.*

We must not forsake our calling for an easy believism. If we do, we will become mere beauticians for those who are dead in trespasses and sins. Not only that, but our very souls will be at stake when we begin to substitute a lie for the truth. The message of sin cannot be hidden away in the archives of the Church's ministry or buried beneath a sugarcoated gospel. It is still the reason Jesus died on the cross of Calvary.

Shallowness comes from seeking only to solve the surface-level issues and avoiding the deeper one. We must expose the sin problem that exists in the human heart and offer forgiveness, cleansing, and deliverance through the crucified Christ.

The Christian Church should offer a community experience with God that generates a significant impact on individuals. Our focus on American individualism often obscures this community dimension.

The Disappearance of Sin

by Earle L. Wilson

The local newspaper recently reported that the book, *Whatever Became of Sin?* by Karl Menninger, was checked out of the public library and not returned. It is officially listed as "lost." The disappearance of the book is ironic since, like the book, sin itself has largely disappeared in our day.

Where Did Sin Go?

It started with society's attempt to make sin attractive. This was accomplished by softening the distinction between right and wrong. Then the sexual revolution eliminated the ugliness of adultery and promiscuity by teaching a "feel good" morality. At the same time, fidelity and marriage became as ugly as Cinderella's stepsisters. Value systems became distorted as God was reduced to a doddering grandfather. With His wrath gone, His judgment impaired, His commandments re-written, His moral absolutes dismissed, sin was no longer cosmic evil. Committing sin no longer resulted in dire eternal consequences. At the worst, it became a temporary inconvenience.

Once you have accomplished this makeover of God, you need only to re-adjust your thinking about the things the old, hell-fire-and-brimstone preachers said God didn't approve of. Pornography, once degrading, is now a freedom of speech. Homosexuality used to be a perversion; now it is an alternate lifestyle. Partial birth abortion, that is, delivering a living, helpless infant's torso and limbs, crushing its skull and vacuuming out its brains, is not barbaric infanticide, but a woman's right to choose. Upholding marriage vows has been vetoed by the right to happiness. Crimes are not committed by cold-blooded criminals, but by people who are misunderstood. Amassing money and gadgets at the expense of family, integrity, and principles is no longer greed, but savvy success. Selfishness is personal fulfillment. Sin, the bug-a-boo of earlier age, has gained legitimacy. It is user friendly. If you are open-minded enough and progressive enough, you'll find sin to be rather warm and welcome.

Sin Is Alive and Well

Don't be taken in by such voices clamoring for your attention with a desire to get you out of the antedeluvian age and into this modern age mentality. God's pronouncements against evil cannot be re-written by cultural forces and pseudo-intellectuals. Sin is still ugly, damaging, and eternally damning. It destroys marriages, wrecks families, breaks hearts, injects hatred, contaminates minds, and defiles bodies.

Sin is not lost. It is masquerading under a veil of acceptable terms such as tolerance, freedom, choice, and rights. The library book may be lost, but sin is alive and, unfortunately, well and thriving.

Let us not be deceived by sin's face-lift. Recognize it for what it is and reject it without a hint of compromise.

How long has it been since you heard a sermon about sin? The lack of conviction in our services directly parallels our lack of clear, Biblical preaching about sin. We are not "putting one over on God." He knows what sin is. He has told us in His Word. And He has charged us with the awesome responsibility not only to tell people what it is but to provide the "good news" that He and He alone has both forgiveness for sins committed and cleansing for sin's nature, for all who will receive such grace. Indeed, the wage paid by sin is death while the gift of God, called salvation, is eternal life.

It is an old message, but still true. If it has become dusty, let's dust it off and preach it again with passion and conviction. The Holy Spirit will honor such preaching and such preachers.

Empowered Witnesses

by Paul S. Rees

For every ordained minister, the Church needs a hundred lay witnesses who will communicate the good news, and back it up with their committed lives. When the first Christians got so filled with the Holy Spirit that some local citizens thought them crazy, they made converts right and left, achieving results that a "cultural Christianity," silent and supine, can never approach.

Jesus was pointed about it: *But you will receive power when the Holy Spirit comes on you; and you will be My witnesses in Jerusalem, and in all Judea and Samaria, and to the ends of the earth* (Acts 1:8). Luke was equally pointed in recording the fulfillment of the promise: *All of them were filled with the Holy Spirit and began to speak in other tongues as the Spirit enabled them* (Acts 2:4).

And with that, they were off! Off to disciple winning and life changing and church planting! Before long it was said of them, *These men who have caused trouble all over the world have now come here* (Acts 17:6). The complacent, sterile, nonproductive church member of today is miles apart from the witnessing fellowship that was looked upon as such a revolutionary thing twenty centuries ago.

What to Do?

Are we to conclude that power for a convincing and contagious discipleship has been withdrawn from the Christian community? Who can seriously believe it—or rest content with it? Is it not better to side with a friend who, out of long years of dealing with stumbling, faltering souls says: "I am perfectly sure that spiritual help and power are as available to us as water or electricity?" What, then, are some of the factors that *condition* and *accompany* the release of God's power through the Holy Spirit in the Christian or the Church?

Eagerness

Heading the list, let's put *eagerness. Blessed are those who hunger and thirst!* Vague wishfulness is not enough. Ardent desire is a prerequisite. People who are more interested in learning how to raise rabbits, win prizes with tulips, or play a good hand at canasta, than they are to be channels of converting power to the broken men and women around them should not be surprised if they remain on the list of "non-effectives" in the Church. They should not wonder if the whole vocabulary and spiritual experience of Pentecost remain foreign to them. When desire ravishes us, God's power will reach us.

Openness

Another factor in power-release is *openness*. Vertically, toward God; horizontally, toward people! *We are not withholding our affection from you,* says Paul, *but you are withholding yours from us. As a fair exchange—I speak as to my children—open wide your hearts also* (2 Corinthians 6:12-13).

It isn't that we are *fated* to be spiritually small and ineffectual. We are *contented* to be. Many of us would begin writing a new chapter in our lives if we would break down in two simple ways: First in *praying* our hearts out to God and, second, in *talking* our hearts out to some vital, soul-winning Christian whom we know and respect.

Cleanliness

Next, there is certainly a close relation between released power and *cleanliness* in the life of the Christian. *Come out from it and be pure, you who carry the vessels of the Lord* (Isaiah 52:11). There is a crass hedonism whose chief concern is summed up in the words, "eat, drink, and be merry." But there is a more subtle hedonism that can be gathered up in the magic phrase "peace of mind." Neither one matches the New Testament, where the passion for holiness always gets a higher rating than the quest for happiness. I can count on God to let power loose in my life when I am ready to let something loose—the hurtful habit, the crippling compromise, the unsurrendered ambition, the stubborn resentment to which I have been clinging.

Directedness

Still another factor that makes for spiritual power-release in the life of the witnessing Christian is what may be called *directedness*. That means not using the Spirit's power for our own purposes, but rather, letting the Spirit use us for God's purposes and glory. A whimsical saint was commenting on the scripture (Isaiah 41) in which Israel, having been called a "worm" is told that God will "thresh the mountains." He said: "Of course God can take a worm and thresh a mountain, provided the worm will wiggle when He says wiggle!" Behind the humor is sober reality.

A scientist, whose nominal Christianity had blazed into something splendidly experiential and vital, was just beginning the witnessing life. One night, at two in the morning, an alcoholic was brought to his door. The friend who brought him said, "I know you can help him." Before he left the bedroom there was momentary reluctance in his heart. "Lord," he murmured, half aloud, "is this what I have to do?" His wife responded, "What would Jesus do?"

It was enough. From two o'clock until six, the man worked with this soul whom alcohol had ravaged. Then victory! A beaten, enchained man was born again by the power of God! But the power flowed through a channel that was flexible enough to be directed.

Empowered witnesses! Examine them wherever you find them. You are certain to find that they are eager souls, transparently open, sensitive to sin, and in no mood to compromise with it. They hold their witness not as a monopoly for them to control, but as a trust for the Holy Spirit to manage—and use.

How to Kill the Holiness Message

by J.R. Mitchell

The message of Christian holiness has had severe opposition from its enemies, but it has probably suffered far more at the hands of friends. The fact that neither friends nor enemies have been able to destroy this biblical truth shows that the message is powerful. But, just for the sake of argument, how might a well-intentioned holiness preacher kill the holiness message?

Tie the Message to Cultural Trends

Perhaps the easiest way to nullify the holiness message is to identify it with passing cultural or social trends. It's tragic that many sincere people have identified this sublime truth with their own narrow, provincial concept of the Christian life. They have insisted on dating or localizing the message by associating it with the spiritual mores of their own region, or the prejudices of some dominant personality. But the message of the holy life belongs to no movement, knows no geographic boundaries, and is not tied to any particular political or cultural pattern.

Express It in Obscure Terms

Another way to kill the holiness message is to express it in obscure biblical language. No one can object to the use of biblical terms. But most people today are either too ignorant of the Bible to know what these terms mean, or they have nothing in their experience with which to relate them. *Crossing the Jordan, the land of milk and honey, chasing out the Amalekites*: These phrases are meaningful to those who are familiar with traditional holiness teaching. But they mean little or nothing to today's youth, who are wondering how they can get through the day without compromising their Christian witness.

Again, the message can be killed by failure to relate it to today's situation. Many of our horse-and-buggy illustrations and our threadbare clichés might as well be dropped. For those of us over fifty, this will not be easy, but it will be highly profitable, both for us, and for those to whom we minister. Fresh language is not a substitute for a fresh message, but it helps.

The present generation is not bothered with breaking clotheslines, kicking cows, or even flat tires. They do not relate to railroads, steam engines, or "the old ship of Zion." They are not really interested in "dwelling under cloudless skies," nor do they hunger for "luscious fruit delectable that grow everywhere." They will be happy if no nuclear bomb breaks over their heads and if they have enough to satisfy their hunger. They know, as a former generation should have known, that these expressions may express a passing phase of the Christian life, but that they do not express all, or even most of it. They know that living the Christian life today requires a down-to-earth approach. What they want is to find an inner resource that will help them to live like Christ in the midst of a sex-crazed, hedonistic age. That resource is the Holy Spirit! They must be told that the eternal yet contemporary Spirit is meaningful today, and not just in a time gone by.

We must be reminded that this age is the vehicle of the Holy Spirit's work, and that the supreme demonstration of the fact that *Jesus Christ is the same yesterday, today and forever* is in His ability to make men and women in His own image.

Insist that a Single Experience Makes One Holy

If this holiness message is to live, we must insist that, however important an experience may be, it is only the beginning of a new life and must always lead to a growing relationship with Christ. To state without qualification that a spiritual experience will end the quest for holiness is to leave a multitude of souls in frustration and defeat. In that condition, they aren't likely to seek any further revelation of the Spirit. There must be an experience of holiness. But it must never be an end in itself or a pattern by which to judge others. The plain truth is that an experience of sanctification does nothing of lasting value unless it is followed by disciplined living. It is a relationship with the living Christ, through the Holy Spirit, that must be emphasized. Then the Christian life will never be static, but always growing and more satisfying.

There is probably no more effective way to destroy the holiness message than by leaving the impression that a second trip to the altar will solve all, or most, of one's spiritual problems. Any intelligent Christian knows that there are areas of need that can only be met over time, through the guidance of Scripture and the help of the Holy Spirit. This doesn't mean that the altar cannot have a meaningful place in one's spiritual growth. But it does mean that the confession, commitment, and openness to the Holy Spirit that takes place there is what really matters. It is the joyful response of the yielded soul that brings God's response, not the coercion of others.

Turn It Inward

To kill the holiness message, it may only be necessary to proclaim it in such a way that it leads to a life of subjective, introspective self-analysis. *Am I sanctified?* may be a legitimate question. But what is not legitimate is constant self-analysis that weakens the spirit and stifles the expression of praise. The tension between what we are and what we will be is a fact that every Christian must learn to live with. The sanctified life must be turned outward, not inward. It must not luxuriate in its own moods while a suffering world is crying out for acts of love and words of hope. Christian holiness must never be separated from the anguish of the oppressed or the hunger of the starving. We need more holiness preaching. But that holiness must be related to the whole of life, socially, spiritually, and racially.

The Holy Spirit is our eternal contemporary. He constantly seeks to help us live holy and productive lives. He is not surprised by any modern innovation and He is not nonplussed by any new form of sin. The Holy Spirit is a creative Spirit, strengthening every yielded soul. He is at home in the office, the classroom, and the kitchen. He haunts the skid rows, the prisons, and the never-never land of the drug addict, seeking to draw everyone to the Savior of men. So let's proclaim the presence and power of the Holy Spirit. And let us never forget that He leads us straight to Christ and the souls of others.

Holiness Is a Social Gospel

by Marlin Hotle

As a child, I sat by my grandfather's side at the Cumberland Grove Wesleyan Camp and listened intently as the evangelist lectured on the Christian's responsibility to care for a needy world. I remember my confusion when, after the service, I heard someone comment disgustedly, "That evangelist doesn't preach holiness. He preaches a *social gospel.*"

I didn't understand his comments then. But as I've grown older, I have come to realize that many in our movement are afraid of any preaching that assigns social responsibility to them. Holiness, to them, is "coming out" instead of "going out." They think it's necessary to wrap pious robes around themselves as if they were in danger of losing their purity by stooping to eat with sinners. I'm not convinced that this kind of purity is worth keeping.

Wesleyan Holiness Is "Social"

The holiness that John Wesley preached—the kind that caused the early Wesleyan Methodists to wage war against slavery and the Pilgrim Holiness folks to begin their many inner-city missions during the 1930s and '40s—was a "social holiness." In the preface to his book, *Hymns and Sacred Poems,* Wesley stated, "The gospel of Christ knows of no religion but social; no holiness but social holiness."

We holiness people find it easy to preach against abortion, and a few may even be moved to picket the abortion mills. That's fine. But real holiness opens her arms to care for the pregnant teen or to minister to the woman who is suffering from the scars of the abortion nightmare. Holiness people often decry the abuses of the welfare system. I have no problem with that. But real holiness feeds the hungry and clothes the naked. True holiness visits the fatherless and weeps with those in prison. God's holiness works for social justice.

True Holiness Results in Action

Don't get me wrong. I am not advocating that we earn our holiness by acts of mercy, or that we will ever save the world through social activity. What I advocate is that the Wesleyan message is one of perfect love, a love that is not only made perfect toward God, but also toward others. This kind of love is not proven by words, but by actions. Just as sure as it will demonstrate itself by the purity of our thoughts and actions before God, so it will be seen in our genuine concern for the spiritual and social well-being of those around us. While it has been nearly 2000 years since the apostle first made the observation, it is still true that the only evidence by which the world judges our faith is our love.

Many years have passed since I heard that critic's comment, but it lingers in my mind. If I were to hear him make that remark today, my response would be, "Sir, holiness *is* a social gospel."

Communicating Holiness Cross-Culturally

by John Connor

In a conference on evangelizing ethnic America, C. Peter Wagner pointed out that Anglos now comprise only about 30 percent of America's population. Further, minorities are now a majority in at least 25 major cities. That means that your neighbor is an ethnic minority. *You are too.* When you consider those facts, it seems clear that our old ways of thinking about culture no longer fit.

Let's consider cross-cultural communication of the holiness message. In our mini-worlds today, any communication outside our own families or community cliques is cross-cultural communication. Another language is not necessary. But there are some basic points we'll need to remember if we are to be good cross-cultural communicators.

"Why" Matters More than "How"

The first thing we must get clear is why we want to communicate. If we understand the *why* of communication, then the *how* becomes easier. In Philippians 1:15-17, Paul lists a number of poor reasons for communicating the gospel, like envy, rivalry, and selfish ambition. Here are some other negative reasons.

Paternalism. This is the "big daddy" concept. It means looking down on the "little people" with our tremendous knowledge and insight. Paternalism says, "I have an enlightened doctrine of sound logical and theological significance." This "sound logic" is generally culture-bound, sometimes coming out of our Christian ghettos.

Theological Purism. This viewpoint seeks to protect orthodoxy, which, by itself, is not bad. But sometimes the orthodoxy that we guard is a particular *form* rather than a particular *meaning.* One theologian calls this "hardening of the categories."

When it comes to holiness, the way we have always said it is "sanctification." Sanctification means perfection. Perfection means sanctification. But we haven't really said anything! Orthodoxy is not a particular way of saying something. It is a particular way of believing.

Guarding the Border. We sometimes think that when it comes to holiness we must, by all means, keep out the charismatics, and the Calvinists, and the liberals. Are we more concerned with who we keep out than who we bring in? In guarding the borders so tightly we may be keeping out sinners who need our message.

The Gospel Is Incarnational

A few weeks ago, while reading Ephesians 5:8, I thought that the translation I was using was mistaken. But I went to another English translation and it said the same thing. So I dug out my Greek text to see how the original language reads. It said the same: *You are light in the Lord.* Charles Kraft calls this "the incarnational gospel." To the people around us, we either become the light or else there is no light.

Communicating, especially communicating cross-culturally, cannot start with duty. To be effective, it must start with love. Social psychologist Stephen Bochner, in a book entitled *Cultures in Contact* says, "To blur the distinction between 'us' and 'them' requires that people become partially 'them,' i.e., incorporate some of 'their' characteristics without, however, losing their own identity."

With this in mind we need to ask, "How badly do we want to communicate?" There is a cost to incarnation. In order for Christ to be incarnate, He had to give up what He valued. I am not sure we understand all that this involves. Jesus *made Himself nothing* (Philippians 2:7). That is the principle of the incarnation.

John gives an example of this in 1 John 3:17. He says that when someone is in need, the loving response is to share one's material possessions with him or her. The incarnational gospel is a person-to-person, face-to-face kind of thing. Communication comes from a relationship where one life is lived in close proximity, in fact, intertwined with another.

How great is our motivation to communicate? Is it great enough to present the gospel incarnationally? *You are light.*

Cross-Cultural Communication Is Difficult

From a logical perspective, cross-cultural communication is just about impossible. There are so many barriers! For instance, if you are in a Zulu home in South Africa, and your teacup is half full, you must never ask to have it filled. That communicates greed. It must be completely empty before you ask for more. Every missionary has some story of cross-cultural bloopers committed with good motives. So how can you communicate to someone from a different culture without making mistakes? You can't. But you can communicate cross-culturally in spite of the difficulty. Here are some pointers.

Expect to look stupid. When communicating cross-culturally, you can expect to do something silly. But here's another rule: You can commit all kinds of cultural blunders and get by with them *if* your person-to-person relationships are sound. If they are not sound, then your first cultural blunder will be suspect, and your second will be seen as intentional. At that point, cross-cultural communication will cease.

Start with your own experience. Teaching something you don't know is like coming back from someplace you've never been. Not long ago I saw an overweight man wearing a huge red button that said, "Ask me how to lose weight." I didn't. You cannot communicate something that you have not experienced. Years ago, an old preacher told some of us young, aspiring pulpiteers never to preach anything that we hadn't lived for six months. In cross-cultural communication, that should be a firm rule.

Dump your theological tomes. At least drop the verbiage. Every kind of discipline has a developed set of technical language, theology included. That's why I like to hear new Christians testify. They don't say it in the way that we always say it!

Within holiness circles we also have developed a set of technical lingo. We usually feel vulnerable when we get away from it. Some time ago I wrote a book on Wesleyan theology for Third World pastors. Before publication the manuscript had to be edited by theologians. Although there was great sympathy for the reason behind my use of simple language, there was also resistance. We like our big words. And when they get broken down into simple terms that everyone understands, but which may not contain the minute theological implications, we feel naked.

Focus on the concrete. Americans love abstract philosophical concepts. I was teaching a class on cults in an African Bible school in Zambia when the Jonestown incident took place. I felt that this was a perfect time to gather up all of the *Time* and *Newsweek* magazines so that my students could make reports. I hounded every mission home in the area, gathering all the magazines I could find. I sorted the articles and assigned them to my students. It soon became evident that these students, though very proficient in English, could not understand the abstract terms used in the articles. Sentences like, "We came floating in over the trees to see the flood of color like cars parked on a great parking lot, only to come to realize that these were actually bodies," did not make a bit of sense. It uses too many abstract images. The reporter was obviously in an airplane and the display of color was, of course, the clothing of the dead. But to my African students, the writing might as well have been Sanskrit. They needed concrete terms.

When was the last time you heard someone preaching holiness by using a concrete example rather than theory? It's almost impossible to communicate pure theory accurately in a cross-cultural setting unless you have a profound understanding of the target culture. But ideas like uncontrolled anger, gossip, forgiveness, or lack of forgiveness can be expressed in concrete terms. Trust the Holy Spirit to work out the theory in the hearts of the sanctified.

Emphasize experience. I once boarded a crowded Korean bus and worked my way to a seat in the back. Soon a young Korean woman, who had attended some Bible studies I'd conducted, also boarded the bus. She saw me and began to push her way back through the crowd to get to where I was. We greeted each other in Korean, but she soon began using vocabulary that I hadn't learned. I was sure that she was telling me about the in-filling of the Spirit in her own life, but my grasp of the language was not great enough to understand her. She kept asking me if I understood, and I kept telling her, "I think I do." Her face brightened and she began to sing one of Charles Wesley's songs about the blessing of the Spirit.

The people who were crowded around may have been shocked, and they probably didn't understand her testimony much better than I did. But they could understand her experience. Focus on experience, not on theory.

Illustrate. If you haven't illustrated, then you probably haven't communicated. If you can't illustrate, you may not have anything to say anyway!

Don't get hung up on terms. Not long ago, I was handed a gospel tract that explained "union life." As I read it, I discovered that it was simply the doctrine of holiness explained by a Baptist! Are our terms sacred, or is the experience sacred? I believe it is more important that people have the experience than that they use the right words.

Depend on the Holy Spirit. This should be obvious. When we realize that we are entering territory where our righteous actions can be misunderstood, where our good motives may be coupled with blunders, and where the value of the gospel will be judged by our witness, then we must depend upon the Holy Spirit.

Communicating cross-culturally is a risky thing. But the world in which we live demands it. The Church can no longer expect to grow mono-culturally. We'll either communicate cross-culturally or stagnate. *You are light in the Lord.* Shine!

Expectation

Seekers after holiness stands in an uneasy position. On the one hand, they have believed the terrifying truth that *without holiness no one will see the Lord.* Yet their own attempts at self-righteousness convince them of the impossibility that holiness could come from their own efforts. God demands holiness. Human beings cannot make themselves holy. Caught between these truths, many seekers have opted for hypocrisy or despair.

This should never be. Holiness is neither a threat to the seeker nor a pillow for the saint. Sanctification should neither intimidate nor insulate. Rather it should be a continual state of seeking after God and His righteousness.

Are we under obligation to pursue holiness? Without doubt. But we do so in the joyful expectation that *he who began a good work in [us] will carry it on to completion until the day of Christ Jesus.* It is God who promises holiness in Christ Jesus. And we have every confidence that, later or sooner, He will honor His word.

Jesus, Thine All-Victorious Love

Jesus, Thine all victorious love
shed in my heart abroad;
then shall my feet no longer rove,
rooted and fixed in God.

O that in me the sacred fire
might now begin to glow,
burn up the dross of base desire,
and make the mountains flow!

O that it now from heav'n might fall,
and all my sins consume!
Come, Holy Ghost, for Thee I call;
Spirit of Burning, come!

Refining Fire, go thro' my heart;
Illuminate my soul.
Scatter Thy life thro' every part,
and sanctify the whole.

—Charles Wesley

Hungering for Holiness

by Roy S. Nicholson

Blessed are those who hunger and thirst for righteousness, for they will be filled—Matthew 5:8

Holiness and blessedness! Holiness and happiness! Holiness and soul health! Holiness sustains a vital relationship to each of them in this day of intense quests for the secret of happiness, blessedness, and success. Bookshelves are filled with volumes on how to achieve success and happiness by self-help.

The world is concerned over the horrible plight of starving millions in famine-plagued lands. Long-continued starvation has produced health conditions that call for immediate action. The response to appeals for public help is amazingly liberal. Yet the starvation continues, because the roots of the problem have not been removed. The public concern over world hunger may diminish, but man persists in the pursuit of happiness through personal positions and possessions. Soul health is neglected, but physical fitness is promoted vigorously. Soul health (true holiness) is the eternal basis of blessedness. Without holiness, all other achievements are but empty husks, which can never satisfy the soul.

A Sweet Invitation

According to John Wesley, the Beatitudes contain "a sweet invitation to true holiness and happiness." In Wesley's *Explanatory Notes on the New Testament,* he called attention to the method that Jesus used in this passage where, instead of "the lofty style, in positive commands, He, in a more gentle and engaging way, insinuates His will and our duty, by pronouncing those happy who comply with it."

In this part of the Sermon on the Mount, our Lord is concerned with "removing the hindrances to true religion." Pride is removed by poverty of spirit. Levity and thoughtlessness are displaced by holy mourning; and anger, impatience, and discontent are healed by Christian meekness. "And once these hindrances are removed, these evil diseases of the soul, which were continually raising false cravings therein, and filling it with sickly appetites, the native appetite of a heaven-born spirit returns; it hungers and thirsts after righteousness: and 'blessed are they . . . for they shall be filled'" (Wesley, *Works,* V:267).

This hunger and thirst are the strongest of all the desires of the true child of God. Such desires can be satisfied by nothing other than spiritual food and drink. Any substitute leads to spiritual death.

The True Objective

In the scripture before us, our Lord sets forth the secret of true blessedness: righteousness, which Mr. Wesley described as "true religion, the image of God, the mind which was in Christ Jesus. It is every heavenly and holy temper in one; springing from, as well as terminating in, the love of God, as our Father and Redeemer, and the love of all men for His sake" (Wesley, *Works,* V:267). The reality of this blessedness is divinely assured to be gloriously possible: *they will be filled.*

The implications of such blessedness involve more than separation from things unclean. All evil must be cleansed from the heart (Matthew 5:8) and one must walk as Christ walked (1 John 2:6). There will be the possession of the other qualities mentioned in the Beatitudes. Blessedness involves both an inward and outward relationship to God and man. It is true holiness that produces peace and joy (Romans 14:17-18; 15:13). This peace and joy are God-given, and the world cannot take them away.

We live in a world where peace and safety seem to hang in the balances. But as God's child, one can have a supernatural sensation and a divine taste of the powers of the world to come, which the natural man does not know, because they are spiritually discerned. Such is the peace that banishes all fear (1 John 4:17-18), as well as doubts that destroy faith.

The Divine Creator designed man for holiness and happiness, but sin marred the man. Christ came to redeem man and to make it possible for man to live in a harmonious relationship to God and his fellowmen. Man has within him an innate instinct that drives him to hunger and thirst for blessedness. Because Satan has beguiled him into seeking it where it cannot be found, man has failed to achieve that for which he hungers and thirsts.

The righteousness that the Beatitudes commend is referred to in the parable of the wedding garment (Matthew 22:11-14). Paul also shows it to be available to believers through faith in the Lord Jesus Christ (1 Corinthians 1:30). A study of John Wesley's observations on this matter will clear the minds of many who may have confused ideas on the question of holiness, without which no man will see the Lord (Hebrews 12:14).

The righteousness of Christ is undoubtedly necessary for any soul who enters into glory. But so is personal holiness, for every child of man. But it is important to observe that they are necessary in different respects. The former is necessary to *entitle* us to heaven, the latter to *qualify* us for it. Without the righteousness of Christ, we would have no *claim* to glory; without holiness we could have no *fitness* for it. By the former we become members of Christ, children of God, and heirs of the kingdom of heaven. By the latter "we are made meet partakers of the inheritance of the saints in light" (Wesley, *Works,* VII:314).

Why this Hunger?

God created man in His own image so that man might glorify God and enjoy Him forever. He created man with the capacity for holiness (Matthew 5:8, 48; 1 Peter 1:15-16). Man may be holy if he wills to be holy. His humanity is no barrier to holiness. The true believer in Christ craves God's best for each area of his life—as it relates to God and man and the church, which is the body of Christ. Thus, a lack of hunger and thirst after righteousness indicates a lack of proper concern for God's purpose in creating man, and an inordinate, depraved appetite for self-interests.

Hungering and thirsting after righteousness demonstrates a desire to achieve personal holiness. Man cannot heal himself of the sin virus. He cannot, by himself, destroy those things that war against his total abandonment of himself to the entire will of God. He cannot be filled (experience the blessedness that Christ promised in Matthew 5:6) until he is enabled by the Holy Spirit to say (and to mean it!): "Your will be done."

This *hunger and thirst after righteousness* reveals a fervent personal desire to participate in Christ's world-encompassing program of evangelism instead of being satisfied to remain a temple-treader in the heartless routine of ritualism. Much more is being said about the *methods* of evangelism than about divine *motivation* for soul winning. There is a real need for a program of discipleship. But one cannot neglect the practice of personal spiritual discipline in order to "be filled" with "righteousness, and peace, and joy in the Holy Spirit." For *anyone who serves God in this way is pleasing to God and approved by men* (Romans 14:18). Thus, by divine enabling, one develops a symmetrical spiritual life. (See 2 Peter 1:1-8.)

A lack of *hunger and thirst after righteousness* calls for serious self-examination. Have I been beguiled into a quest for that which dulled my interests and interfered with my relationship with God? Have I allowed my sense of values to become so distorted that I overvalue things that gratify self and undervalue things that glorify God? Have I permitted position, promotion, and possessions to become my criteria of blessedness and happiness, instead of that which pleases God? Have those things dulled my hunger for that which enriches the spiritual life?

Pause and Remember

Let us pause to remember—to call to mind things that were once regarded as of vital importance but that are now dismissed or forgotten. It might astonish one to discover how often the Bible contains the admonition to remember what once had been well known.

Remember the purpose of God in man's creation, the provision for man's redemption, the promises of God to man, the prayers for man, the power of God to accomplish His purpose for man's holiness and happiness, and the testimonies of those who have experienced the blessed satisfaction of His heart-cleansing fullness, as Mrs. Clara Teare Williams' joyous song of testimony, "Satisfied," witnesses:

"Hallelujah! I have found Him—Whom my soul so long has craved!

Jesus satisfies my longing, Through His blood I now am saved."

Remembering this, let us accept God's sweet invitation to true holiness and happiness. What a difference it will make!

A Plea and Prayer
for Holiness

by David S. Medders

Recently, I have reflected on my own passionate proclamation of holiness, the doctrine and experience, promises and power. I love to preach holiness. And my thoughts have gone further, back to my childhood growing up in a holiness church, to my early conversion, call to ministry, and total surrender in sanctification. I have asked myself, "What was the essence of the holy life that I saw in certain individuals around me that convinced me of the reality of holiness?" I can still remember so clearly the song, "It's real, it's real, oh, I know it's real! Praise God, the doubts are settled, for I know, I know it's real!" My young heart was deeply convicted by the sanctifying power of the Holy Spirit when I compared the striving after God that I knew with the fullness of God that I saw in the lives of many wonderful saints.

Captured by Example

My heart was captured by the desire to be holy, as Christ was, when I saw living saints around me. I couldn't deny the lifestyles that I saw. My only explanation for them was that a holy God lived in these people in a way that was so real and attractive that I thought I would die if I did not experience it too. That was my passion 29 years ago when I knelt in the sawdust at a camp meeting altar and cried out to God for His sanctifying presence. Today I ask myself, "What was the essence of those holy lives that embodied the doctrine and won my heart?" I'm not interested in the external characteristics of their ages and cultures, but in the timeless touches of heaven that told me God was holy, and helped me see Him clearly.

The greatest example to my young eyes was a man whom we children knew as Papa Shigley. There was such a holy presence in his spirit. Later I would see it again so clearly in Dr. Roy S. Nicholson.

I wonder, do my three sons, now 18, 15, and 13, see in me the essence of holiness that was so real in these saintly men? Am I faithfully passing on what I have received—the richness of a holy life, filled with the presence of God?

In a broader sense, I ask, "As holiness people, what are we passing on to the next generation?" Beyond the clear preaching of doctrine and a call to the experience of holiness, what will be our legacy? Frankly, I wonder about the quality of holiness that we are reproducing. Do we continue to be holiness people simply because of our commitment to a doctrine, or do we have among us living examples of the fullness of Christ and of His holy presence?

Here are two of the fundamental characteristics that I have seen in holy lives.

Life of Love

First, they exuded a love for God and others that was warm, genuine, fervent, and tender. I can still see faces filled with the glow of the love of God and warm fellowship. Even as a child, I knew when God was present, and I loved it.

When I read in Scripture about a most excellent way that was patient and kind, I knew what it looked like. These people were not envious, boastful or proud; nor rude, self-seeking or easily angered. They could forgive and forget. They rejoiced in the Lord and were full of hope, trust, and perseverance. They cared and cried. They were real men and women with a real experience of a real and loving God. I could see it, taste it, feel it. I knew it was genuine, and it made my heart hungry.

Today, I wonder if that is the holiness that our young people see in us. Is anyone pursuing holiness because of the overwhelming evidence of the love of God in our lives? I feel the sting of John the Beloved who wrote:

> *Do not love the world or anything in the world. If anyone loves the world, the love of the Father is not in him. For everything in the world—the cravings of sinful man, the lust of his eyes and the boasting of what he has and does—comes not from the Father but from the world. The world and its desires pass away, but the man who does the will of God lives forever* (1 John 2:15-17).

Did you hear it? If anyone loves the world, the love of the Father is not in him. Cravings, lust, and boasting of what one has and does come *from the world.*

What are our greatest pursuits? What consumes our conversations at home and on the job? What describes our priorities and stewardship? Is it the pursuit of God? And is the genuineness of our example causing others to pursue Him too?

Life of Humility

The second characteristic that I have seen in the holy life is humility. I could not have expressed it back then, but this mark stands out clearly in my memory: the saints I knew in my childhood walked humbly before God and others.

Yes, they lived simple lives without many of the world's trappings. And yes, I think they would be astounded by the affluence of present-day Christians. They might be impressed at how much God has blessed us. But would they be impressed by the things of our spirit— our humble walk before God with reverence and appropriate fear— or would they see a trampling of His courts?

John the Beloved indicated the bridge between these two traits, declaring that boasting of what one has and does is a deadly reflection of the love of the world. James continues the theme: *Now listen, you who say, "Today or tomorrow we will go to this or that city, spend a year there, carry on business and make money." . . . Instead, you ought to say, "If it is the Lord's will, we will live and do this or that." As it is, you boast and brag. All such boasting is evil* (James 4:13-16).

I do not cast stones or pronounce judgment, except upon my own life. I'm simply asking, "Does our holiness reflect godly humility?" Would this mark of godliness be identified by our children as something that drew them to Christ and holy living?

Our forebearers knew a Christ who invited, Take My yoke upon you and learn from Me, for I am gentle and humble in heart, and you will find rest for your souls (Matthew 11:29). They reflected a Christ who humbled Himself and became obedient to death—even death on a cross! (Philippians 2:8). Their holiness preaching always included a call to humility, and their vision was the same as that of Paul, who cried out, *Be completely humble and gentle; be patient, bearing with one another in love* (Ephesians 4:2). Revival appeals usually began with a call to repent and the promise that God would move only when His people humbled themselves (2 Chronicles 7:14).

Holiness of Today

My perception may be wrong, but what I see today is a much more strident holiness, more comfortable, almost smug in its blessings, out of touch with the poor, strong willed, adept at exercising power, and enjoying the tokens of position and success. The question, it seems, is not whether these things are wrong, but whether or not we walk humbly before God.

The prophet declared: *This is the one I esteem: he who is humble and contrite in spirit and trembles at My word* (Isaiah 66:2). James warned:

> *God opposes the proud, but gives grace to the humble* (James 4:6). *Humble yourselves before the Lord, and He will lift you up* (James 4:10). *Who is wise and understanding among you? Let him show it by his good life, by* deeds done in the humility that comes from wisdom. *But if you harbor bitter envy and selfish ambition in your hearts, do not boast about it or deny the truth. Such "wisdom" does not come down from heaven, but is earthly, unspiritual, of the devil* (James 3:13-15, emphasis added).

The grave danger is not in perverting holiness, but forgetting the fact that *God opposes the proud* (James 4:6). He flatly promises that *whoever exalts himself will be humbled* (Matthew 23:12). Those are profound warnings of the danger of pride.

C. S. Lewis wrote in his famous *Screwtape Letters*, "We must picture hell as a state where everyone is perpetually concerned about his own dignity and advancement, where everyone has a grievance, and where everyone lives the deadly serious passions of envy, self-importance and resentment."

Today I honor the holiness of our forefathers that was distinguished by the presence of Christ expressed in genuine love and humility. That was the convincing reality that drew me to a sanctifying experience of God and imprinted the truth of the doctrine of holiness upon my life. My hope is that we will pursue and proclaim a holiness that is alive with the presence of God, attractive, contagious. More than that, I plead before God to renew His Church in these days, and I pray that my life will daily reflect all that I have seen, tasted, and know to be the holiness of God.

Man has a double need—his sinful acts need pardon; his sinful nature needs cleansing, changing, purifying. Holiness is not freedom from mistakes, from infirmity, or from temptation. It is not a state or grace from which one cannot fall, nor a state in which further advance is impossible.

—William Booth

Is It for Me?

A Paraphrase from J.A. Wood's Perfect Love

by Martha M. Evans

I s holiness for me? Everyone admits that we are bound to aim at holiness. But can I, a garden variety, born-again Christian, expect a second work of sanctifying grace subsequent to regeneration? My Bible supports at least a dozen reasons why we may confidently believe that a purified, sin-free life is our Lord's intention for every Christian.

God expressly commands it. The Lord commanded Moses to tell Israel, *Be holy because I, the Lord your God, am holy* (Leviticus 19:2). Jesus told His hearers, *Be perfect, therefore, as your heavenly Father is perfect* (Matthew 5:48). Does God command the impossible? Would our Lord give us orders we could not follow? You know He would not.

The Bible warns us to be holy. Paul exhorts us, *Since we have these promises, dear friends, let us purify ourselves from everything that contaminates body and spirit, perfecting holiness out of reverence for God* (2 Corinthians 7:1). God bases His requirements for human beings on what it is possible for us to do through God's grace. Remember it: God requires no impossibilities.

Holiness Is Promised

Holiness is expressly promised in Scripture. *I will save you from all your uncleanness* (Ezekiel 36:29). Does God mean to tease us by such promises, while keeping the full cleansing of holiness out of reach?

What God commands, He promises to aid us in doing. In the case of holiness, a whole series of commands and promises are correlated to each other. They are summed up in the command, *I am*

God Almighty; walk before Me and be blameless (Genesis 17:1). A correlated promise is, *My grace is sufficient for you* (2 Corinthians 12:9). The Lord never asks us to do something without promising the grace necessary to perform it.

Scripture repeatedly declares the possibility of attaining full holiness. (1 Corinthians 1:30; Ephesians 4:24; and 1 Thessalonians 3:13).

Christ, the apostles, and the inspired authors of the Bible made holiness the subject of definite, fervent prayer. If they did not believe holiness to be attainable, would they have prayed for it? (Psalm 51:10; Matthew 6:13; John 17:17; and 1 Thessalonians 5:23).

Holiness Is Taught

Holiness is taught in the Bible as having been experienced. Zechariah and Elizabeth are described as *upright in the sight of God, observing all the Lord's commandments and regulations blamelessly* (Luke 1:6).

God made provision in the atonement, for the entire sanctification of Christians. Christ *bore our sins in His body on the tree, so that we might die to sins and live for righteousness* (1 Peter 2:24).

Holiness is the declared reason why the Holy Spirit dwells in the heart of the Christian. (Ephesians 3:14-19).

The Bible declares the necessity of our full cleansing, points to Christ's blood as the cleansing agent, and to the Holy Spirit as the Person doing the work. (2 Timothy 3:16-17; John 15:3; John 17:17; 2 Thessalonians 2:13).

Holiness is the highest object of Christian ministry. Paul says that the Lord calls persons into various Christian ministries to prepare God's people for works of service . . . until we all reach unity in the faith and become mature, attaining to the whole measure of the fullness of Christ (Ephesians 4:12-13).

Holiness Is Attainable

If holiness is not attainable, why make vigorous and prayerful efforts to be holy? To aim at a state, without the expectation of reaching it, is a hard task. In what other field of endeavor in life is it considered efficient to strive toward something that you know at the outset is unattainable?

God's Call to Purity

by Melvin H. Snyder

We hear a lot about love these days—God's love. "Smile," says a familiar expression, "God loves you." Indeed, God does love us. Calvary is love's supreme expression. Christ died for all because His love, unmistakably, extends to all. What a message to proclaim! We are commissioned to carry it to all people everywhere. It is the "good news" which obligates us to every person. How tragic that anyone should not hear! But does our responsibility end there? It does not. We are to further teach them *everything [God has] commanded you* (Matthew 28:20).

Recently, I have been reading and rereading Paul's first letter to the infant church at Thessalonica—a church that was born out of Paul's own proclamation of the "good news." Upon hearing the good news, they *turned from idols to serve the true living God* (1 Thessalonians 1:9b, Phillips). Having moved to other fields of labor, Paul, at a distance, felt burdened for them; so much so that he could not refrain from sending a letter to them, by the hands of Timothy. And what was the burden of the letter? Let Paul speak for himself:

> *Finally, brothers, we instructed you how to live in order to please God, as in fact you are living. Now we ask you and urge you in the Lord Jesus to do this more and more. For you know what instructions we gave you by the authority of the Lord Jesus. It is God's will that you should be sanctified: that you should avoid sexual immorality; that each of you should learn to control his own body in a way that is holy and honorable, not in passionate lust like the heathen, who do not know God; and that in this matter no one should wrong his brother or take advantage of him. The Lord will punish men for all such sins,*

as we have already told you and warned you. For God did not call us to be impure, but to live a holy life. Therefore, he who rejects this instruction does not reject man but God, who gives you His Holy Spirit (1 Thessalonians 4:1-8).

Evangelism Is a Call

Paul makes it clear that evangelism is more than enunciating the good news of God's redeeming love and the forgiveness of sins through faith in Christ. It is also a clarion call to holiness of heart and life— "The calling of God is not to impurity but to the most thorough purity." This, without question, is the crux of Paul's burden for the Thessalonian Christians. And note that the exhortation is to Christians and not to "heathen, who do not know God." It is significant that Paul finds it unnecessary to write to them about some things. For one thing, he says it is unnecessary to write to them about love. *Now about brotherly love we do not need to write to you, for you yourselves have been taught by God to love each other. And in fact, you do love all the brothers throughout Macedonia* (1 Thessalonians 4:9-10).

For another thing, Paul says it is unnecessary to write to them about the Second Coming. *Now, brothers, about times and dates we do not need to write to you, for you know very well that the day of the Lord will come like a thief in the night* (1 Thessalonians 5:1-2). However, Paul did feel that it was most important to write them about purity of life. Their love, he insists, must be kept pure by the indwelling Holy Spirit. It appears that there was a tendency on the part of some to be lax in this regard, even to make fun of this biblical puritanism. Therefore, he warns, *he who rejects this instruction does not reject man but God, Who gives you His Holy Spirit* (1 Thessalonians 4:8).

Doctrine Is Not Enough

Again, he reminds them that to accept the doctrine of Christ's Second Coming is not enough. Only a holy life could make them ready for that coming, which could happen at any time. So Paul ends this brief letter with a prayer for their entire sanctification. *May God Himself, the God of peace, sanctify you through and through. May your whole spirit, soul and body be kept blameless at the coming of our Lord Jesus Christ* (1 Thessalonians 5:23). Then he adds a word of encouragement that this holy life is not a vain pursuit. *The one who calls you is faithful and He will do it* (1 Thessalonians 5:24).

The times in which we live highlight the need for just such a message. This message must once again be clearly and repeatedly spoken across the Church. As our people are called to holiness, evangelism will take place among us in exact proportion to their response. We are not so much in danger of giving up our written doctrinal position as we are of allowing it to become a "dead letter."

There is absolutely no substitute for a holy life! The Lord of the Church has declared, *Blessed are the pure in heart: for they shall see God.* In time, they shall see Him by the eye of faith. In eternity, they shall see Him face to face and be like Him forever. God's call is to purity; let there be no mistake about it.

Sin must have no triumph; and the Redeemer of mankind must have His glory. But if man be not perfectly saved from all sin, sin does triumph, and Satan exult, because they have done a mischief that Christ either cannot or will not remove. To say He cannot, would be shocking blasphemy against the infinite power and dignity of the great Creator; to say He will not, would be equally such against the infinite benevolence and holiness of His nature.

—Adam Clarke

The Imperative of Entire Sanctification

by Wayne E. Caldwell

Forget about the holiness movement! Forget about any holiness church if you wish (though I hope you will not). You may even forget about some of the "doctrinal" terms that we use, if you must. But there are some things we cannot and must not forget!

What the Bible teaches about sin, and the provision that Jesus made for our sins, cannot be forgotten without fatal loss. Why did God's only Son die? Was it only to save us *in* our sins? Of course not! He died to save us *from* our sins. That is, *to cleanse us from all sin.*

Jesus died for our justification and regeneration. That's biblical. (Romans 3:20-30; 4:25; 5:1-9,18; Galatians 2:16-17; 3:8-11; Titus 3:5-7.) He also died for our sanctification. That's biblical too. (John 17:17-19; 1 Corinthians 1:30; 1 Thessalonians 4:3-4; 5:23-24; Hebrews 10:10-14; 12:14; 13:12.)

Few people have any problem with the fact that we have all sinned and that we need a Savior. We need to be forgiven. We need to be born again. We desperately need for Jesus to save us. That brings a radical change when it happens. But we need something more. (1 Thessalonians 3:9-13; 4:1-8.) We need our very nature and attitude toward God and others to change. We need also to be cleansed. We need to be purged. We need to be purified. We need to be sanctified entirely, completely (1 Thessalonians 5:23-24).

Original Sin

There's something about us that God does not and cannot forgive, because we are not directly responsible for having it. It's the sinful nature that we all have inherited through the human family from Adam. The Bible is explicit at this point. (Romans 5:12-21; 8:6-8; 12:1-2; 1 Corinthians 3:1-4.) Even David had some insight into his sinful nature, as well as being aware of his specific sins of adultery and murder (Psalm 51:1-11).

Complete in Christ

God wants us to be entirely and completely sanctified. That's not forgiveness, or justification, or the new birth. Our new life in Christ is great. It's a tremendous change that occurs when a person is saved. When it happens, we are usually filled with joy. We have a love that we did not have before. We have peace with God. But the work of sanctification has only begun. There is still an attitude that's unlike Christ. It must go!

God, through His Son Jesus, has made it possible for us to be free from all sin—even the inherited kind, for which we are not responsible. A remedy has been provided for our sinful nature. We are responsible to keep our minds and hearts open to the cleansing, purging, refining, purifying power of the Holy Spirit as He applies that remedy to us. That is the imperative of entire sanctification!

The Sanctification of
Dr. E. Stanley Jones

Compiled & Edited by Bernie Smith

After my conversion, which made a decisive change in my life as a young man, I lived in the joy and radiance of that experience for about a year. Then the clouds began to come over me, or, more accurately, the clouds seemed to arise from within. There were depths that this new conversion experience touched and subdued, but did not control and cleanse. There was a dark, ugly something that was not amenable to the new life that had been introduced in conversion. I was a house divided against myself. And I knew I could not stand until I was inwardly unified.

Wanting More

Fortunately, at that time I found a little book in a Sunday school library called *The Christian's Secret of a Happy Life*. When I took it out, I did so with a sense of destiny. I began to read it, and it set my heart on fire to get the type of life shown in its pages. When I got to the forty-second page, the Inner Voice whispered, "Now is the time to get it." But I pleaded that I didn't know what I wanted, that this book was showing me, and that as soon as I finished reading it I would see, and then I could seek intelligently.

But the Voice was imperious: "Now is the time to seek." Apparently God was willing to take me on my half-knowledge, if I would give Him my whole heart. I saw I was in a controversy, so I closed the book, dropped on my knees beside my bed, and said as simply as a child, "Now, Lord, what am I to do?" And He replied, "Will you lay your all upon My altar?" I thought a moment and replied, "Yes, Lord, my all."

Little did I know how much was wrapped up in that "all." It has been unfolding ever since.

Then came the reply. "Then take My all!" I arose and said, "I will! I take Your all!" Little did I know how much was wrapped up in *that* "all." It, too, has been unfolding ever since. And what an "all" it is!

Accepting Everything

I walked around the room, pushing my hands from me, as if I were pushing away doubts that closed in upon me. I did this for about ten minutes, when suddenly I was filled. Wave after wave of refining fire swept through my being: physical, mental, and spiritual. I could only pace the floor with tears of quiet joy streaming down my cheeks. The Holy Spirit had invaded me and taken complete possession. He was cleaning and uniting the depths I could not control. The subconscious mind, which is the special area of the work of the Holy Spirit, was being purified and empowered and united with the conscious mind. So now that subconscious mind and the conscious mind were under a single control—the Holy Spirit. Life was on a permanently higher level.

How Soon?

by Wilbur T. Dayton

Most people would agree that we must be holy to enter heaven. Many believe that the miracle of sanctification occurs at and in the moment of death. The glory of the Wesleyan position is the discovery that it can and should occur earlier than that.

But how much earlier? Have we been too content simply to prove that it can be before death? And have we missed the scriptural indications that it ought to be very near the beginning of the Christian life, providing purity, power, and fullness for a life and service acceptable to God?

Now Is the Time

At Pentecost, Peter did not recommend a long wait. The promise was to all who truly repent and are baptized (Acts 2:38-39). Delay seems unnecessary and dangerous. Wesley argued that "as soon as ever a person is justified" is the "very time preferable to all others" (Letter to T. Rankin, 1774). Delay erodes readiness and endangers one's ever arriving at Christian perfection.

Did only three days elapse between Paul's conversion and his sanctification (being filled with the Holy Ghost)? See Acts 9:3-17. The latter even preceded water baptism, which had not yet been his privilege. In his case, the reality preceded the symbol (Matthew 3:11).

Paul evidently understood that the gift of the Spirit was primarily for the beginning of one's Christian life and not as a certificate of achievement near the end. There are three occasions recorded of Paul's ministry to new believers who had not had the benefit of regular apostolic guidance through the first months of their Christian lives. Each incident is revealing.

Paul met certain young converts at Ephesus and wanted to evaluate their spiritual situation. His chief question was whether they had received this heavenly "gift" since they had become believers (Act 19:2). Not only was their theology (and baptism) brought up to date, but immediately Paul led them into this promised experience.

Later, in the epistle to the Ephesians, Paul speaks freely of this *seal* (1:13), the *deposit guaranteeing our inheritance* (v. 14), the indwelling Spirit, the indwelling Christ, and the fullness of God (3:16-19) as the very essence of victorious living and effective service.

Again, Paul strongly desired to visit Rome, and was delayed. He wrote about the reason for urgency. These people from varied backgrounds had not had regular apostolic ministry—had not likely been led into this experience that is so necessary at the beginning of the Christian life. Paul wanted to share this spiritual gift (*charisma*) that is provided for establishing them in Christian grace (Romans 1:11). The next verse uses the word for *encouraged* that Jesus used of the Holy Spirit in the fourth gospel. At the third church, Thessalonica, Paul was not able to minister through the early months of its existence and, so, had to fill the gap by epistles. What was the burden of 1 Thessalonians, written only months after spectacular conversions out of raw, though sophisticated, heathenism?

Aside from the rejoicing over their sound conversions, Paul was concerned with what was *lacking in [their] faith* (3:10). The proposed remedy was to *make [their] love increase and overflow for each other* (3:12). The reason was the hope of the Second Coming.

It Is God's Will

This is all explained and illustrated by the will of God—*that you should be sanctified* (4:3)—which is aimed at the successful Christian living to which we are called (verses 7-8). After more elaboration, Paul prays, *May God Himself, the God of peace, sanctify you through and through* (5:23).

With the firm assurance of answered prayer, he continues, *The one who calls you is faithful and He will do it* (5:24). The aorist tense (emphasizing the finished act or event) is used in the Greek for the words *increase, overflow,* and *sanctified,* even when it seems remarkable grammatically. Paul is praying for definite action on God's part.

The second epistle to the Thessalonians, written perhaps three months later, seems to indicate that the prayer was answered. Their love was increasing and they were exhibiting the healthy growth that sanctified ones should have (1:3).

How long must one wait for the gift of the Holy Spirit? Only until he knows the promise and joyfully, expectantly claims it. The abiding Comforter is for the journey of the Christian life, not just for crossing the swollen river of death. Why wait? Ask and receive (Luke 11:13).

Sanctification is that renewal of our fallen nature by the Holy Ghost received through faith in Jesus Christ, whose blood of atonement has power to cleanse from all sin; whereby we are delivered from the guilt of sin, which is justification, but are washed entirely from its pollution and are enabled, through grace, to love God with all our hearts and to walk in his holy commandments blameless.

—Luther Lee

Clean Hands and a Pure Heart

by Barry L. Ross

David asks in Psalm 24:3, *Who may ascend the hill of the Lord? Who may stand in His holy place?* The response is: *He who has clean hands and a pure heart* (24:4). The outward demonstration (clean hands) arises from the inward character (pure heart). But what does it mean to have clean hands and a pure heart?

In his defense against the charge of his three "friends" that he has sinned, the Old Testament character Job declared, *Yet my hands have been free of violence* (Job 16:17). Again he said, *Those with clean hands will grow stronger* (Job 17:9).

Rebellion

Isaiah gives some insight: *When you spread out your hands in prayer, I [the Lord] will hide My eyes from you* (Isaiah 1:15). Why will the Lord hide His eyes? Because *your hands are full of blood* (1:15). God is speaking here to the people of Israel who were citizens of His earthly kingdom.

Why does He speak in such a harsh manner? In Isaiah 1:2, God calls Israel children whom He had brought up. As sons of God, the people of Israel should have been mirrors of God's character—"like father, like son." *But they have rebelled against Me,* says God. Rebellion is an attitude of the heart that evidences itself in our actions. The hands become the symbol for all our actions.

When I was a boy my father had some very strictly enforced rules to govern our household of seven children. One of these was that before every meal, we had to wash our hands. Some ten minutes before the meal was to be ready, my mother would call us to the meal. This gave us time to wash our hands, comb our hair, and prepare ourselves for sitting together as a family to eat. But one of the "sins" I was born with was procrastination. I always believed I had a few more minutes to keep on doing what I was doing and, of course, usually what I was doing made my hands dirty. Suddenly the ten minutes would have passed and the final call for the meal would come.

What to do? There was now no time to wash my hands, for another of my father's rules was that we could not be late in coming to the meal. So I would hurry to the table, hands in my pockets or behind my back, slip into my chair, then hide my hands under the table, while my father said the prayer of thanksgiving.

But how does one eat with his hands under the table? So, hoping to be unnoticed, at the end of my father's prayer, I would slip my hands slowly out from under the table, pick up my fork and knife and commence to eat, all the time trying to hide the palms of my hands from my father's "all-seeing" eyes. Without fail, of course, he would notice the strange way I was eating and would ask, "Barry, did you wash your hands?"

Adding to my sins, I would reply, "Yes." But my father liked to see evidence and would then say, "Show me your hands!"

Sin Increases

With utmost reluctance I would slowly expose my hands for his inspection. And there, right on the palms of my hands, would be the evidence. I had disobeyed (or delayed in obeying) and I had then lied. And the evidence of my sin was on my hands. So long as I could keep my hands hidden I thought the attitude of my heart could not be seen.

So it was with the Israelites, and so it is with all of us. One may think that his evil deeds (resulting from the heart attitude of rebellion) are hidden and, so long as one keeps his hands hidden (In the pockets? Behind one's back?), the "evidence" of one's sins is hidden even from himself.

But in a moment of forgetfulness the unrepentant one spreads his hands open before the Lord in some prayer of supplication. As he opens his hands, there on his palms appear the unwashed stains of his sins! And even though one multiplies prayers God *will not listen* (Isaiah 1:15).

Cleanliness Demanded

Is there no remedy? With such "bloodstained" hands is there no way I can become acceptable before God? "Yes, yes," says the Lord. *Wash and make yourselves clean. Take your evil deeds out of My sight* (Isaiah 1:16).

How do I wash myself? By washing my hands? No. By washing my heart. David, in repentance for his double sin of adultery and murder, cried out to the Lord in Psalm 51: *Wash away all my iniquity and cleanse me from my sin* (51:2), *Cleanse me with hyssop, and I will be clean; wash me, and I will be whiter than snow* (51:7), *Blot out all my iniquity* (51:9), and *Create in me a pure heart, O God* (51:10).

O, the wonder of it! When my *heart* has been washed by the blood of Jesus Christ, the bloodstains on my *hands* disappear as though they had never been. *When my heart is pure my hands are clean.* I can open my hands in the very presence of the Lord.

And when the call rings out, *Who may stand in His holy place?*, with confidence, I can reply, "*I* may. By the blood of Jesus Christ, I may." For my heart is pure and my hands are clean.